DICTIONARY *of* GYPSY MYTHOLOGY

"*Dictionary of Gypsy Mythology* by Claude Lecouteux is an eye-opening revelation of the wealth and riches of a people and culture struck by hatred and poverty from their fellow humans due to their needs and ways. A deeply needed recognition and sharing of a group long reviled and antagonized that was able to keep its soul alive in the face of persecution. Truly the heart of the Gypsy is worth its weight in gold. An invaluable history and insight into a unique and strong people."

MAJA D'AOUST, WITCH OF THE DAWN,
COAUTHOR OF *THE SECRET SOURCE,* AND
AUTHOR OF *WHITE WITCH TAROT*

"With the *Dictionary of Gypsy Mythology,* Claude Lecouteux has filled a void long overdue in its need for address. He approaches a mysterious and all too oft misunderstood culture with respect, compassion, and genuine interest. The resulting text is compelling, informative, educational, and practical, as the alphabetical layout lends itself to research as well as reading for pleasure."

VANESSA SINCLAIR, PSY.D., PSYCHOANALYST, ARTIST,
AND AUTHOR OF *SWITCHING MIRRORS*

DICTIONARY
of GYPSY
MYTHOLOGY

**Charms, Rites, and
Magical Traditions of the Roma**

CLAUDE LECOUTEUX

Translated by Jon E. Graham

Inner Traditions
Rochester, Vermont

Inner Traditions
One Park Street
Rochester, Vermont 05767
www.InnerTraditions.com

Originally published in French under the title *Dictionnaire de Mythologie tzigane* by Éditions Imago, 7 rue Suger, 75006 Paris
First U.S. edition published in 2018 by Inner Traditions

Library of Congress Cataloging-in-Publication Data

Names: Lecouteux, Claude, author.
Title: Dictionary of gypsy mythology : charms, rites, and magical traditions of the Roma / Claude Lecouteux.
Other titles: Dictionnaire de mythologie tzigane. English
Description: Rochester, Vermont : Inner Traditions, 2018. | Includes bibliographical references and index.
Identifiers: LCCN 2017044243 (print) | LCCN 2018015966 (e-book) | ISBN 9781620556672 (hardcover) | ISBN 9781620556689 (e-book)
Subjects: LCSH: Romanies—Social life and customs—Dictionaries. | Romanies—Folklore—Dictionaries. | Romanies—Religion—Dictionaries.
Classification: LCC DX157 .L4313 2018 (print) | LCC DX157 (e-book) | DDC 398.2089/91497—dc23
LC record available at https://lccn.loc.gov/2017044243

Printed and bound in the United States by Berryville Graphics, Inc.

10 9 8 7 6 5 4 3 2 1

Text design and layout by Debbie Glogover
This book was typeset in Garamond Premier Pro with Myriad Pro used as a display typeface

Inner Traditions wishes to express its appreciation for assistance given by the government of France through the National Book Office of the Ministère de la Culture in the preparation of this translation.

Nous tenons à exprimer nos plus vifs remerciements au gouvernement de la France et au ministère de la Culture, Centre National du Livre, pour leur concours dans la préparation de la traduction de cet ouvrage.

CONTENTS

THE PEOPLE OF ORAL TRADITION

The Roma (or Romany/Romani, a term that also designates their language)—better known in many countries as "Gypsies"—are a traditionally nomadic people suffering from the inveterate hostility of local populaces who regard them as misfits, intruders, and foreigners. Sedentary peoples have always viewed wanderers with suspicion, and Gypsies have been attributed with every shortcoming over the centuries.[1] They have also been subject to a great deal of persecution.[2] In the eighteenth century Johann Heinrich Zedler (1706–1751), relying mainly on the dissertation of Jacob Thomasius,[3] published a very long entry in his *Universal Dictionary* (*Universallexikon*) summing up what was then known about the Gypsies. In it, he described them as "a heterogeneous group whose distinct features are delinquency and nomadism." In the mid-nineteenth century the Gypsies of Transylvania were allegedly louse-ridden, lazy thieves, but no one could play the *csárdás* (a Hungarian dance) music better, is how the German writer Franz Obert (1828–1908) essentially described them in 1851. At that time the population of Transylvanian Gypsies was estimated at around 750,000, and they pursued a variety of

1

trades,* with these professions being an aspect of their identity. Nevertheless, they led a wretched life, and Engelbert Wittich collected a poem in 1911 that describes their situation.

> *Me hom i tikno, tschorelo Sindenger tschawo.*
> *Mer Dai muies da mer Dad hi stildo.*
> *Gamlo, baro Dewel! Me hom kiake tschorelo*
> *Tta mer Dades ano Stilapen, les hi bokhelo.*
> *Man hi tschi har mer Baschamaskeri.*
> *Me lau la da dschau ani Kertschemi,*
> *Dschin da has i bresla lowe man.*
> *Naschaua pascha mer Dad ano Stilapen,*
> *Djomles gaua lowe, job has froh:*
> *Gana hilo buter kenk bokhelo!*

> I am a poor Gypsy child
> My mother is dead, my father is in prison,
> My God, great God! I am so pure,
> My father is in prison and he is starving.
> I have nothing besides my instrument.
> I take it and go to the inn
> To earn a little money.
> I went to visit my father in prison,
> I gave him some money, and he is content:
> Now he is no longer starving!

All the ethnologists of the eighteenth and nineteenth centuries noted the propensity of the Gypsies for thievery, and in 1868

---

*These included cobblers (*ciobatori*), tinsmiths (*cotorari*), musicians (*ghilabari*), musicians (*lăutari*) and stringed-instrument makers (*cautari*), locksmiths (*mečteri lacatuši*), artisans of wooden objects (*udari, lingurari*), masons (*salahori*), gardeners and farmers (*vatraši*), gold-panners (*zlatari*), bear-tamers (*ursari*), and smiths (*kalderaš*).

The Trades of the Gypsies

Jean-Alexandre Vaillant collected some illuminating evidence of this in the form of a dialogue.

Who do you call *modorons* (*modorani*)?
  Modorons are all the thieves of the highways.
Do they have a god?
  They believe in neither god nor the devil.
Yet it is said that they pray to God?
  Yes, they pray to the god of thieves (*devles čoresks*).
Would you be able to tell me their prayer?
  I can do that for you because I know it, and this is it:

"Divine charity, I beg you to give me everything I ask of you because you are beautiful, great, and strong.

If you permit me to rob the tightwads of their brandy, rogome (*i iagali*), a chicken, a goose, a lamb, a sow, and a cow, I will give you a large candle.

If I steal something and folk come into my home to see what I have stolen to go tell the master, and do not see anything, I will give you two large candles.

If the police come into my house, and then leave because they did not see anything, I will give you three large candles because you are the great trinity."[4]

The poor reputation of the Gypsies is often reflected in the names that were given to them. We may take as an example a name from Norway; here they were called *Skøyer,* meaning "thieves."

Originating in India, as has been shown by studies of their language,*[5] the Gypsies reached Europe in the ninth century and spread across the continent from east to west.

> Byzantium: ninth century
> Crete: 1332
> Corfu: 1346
> Wallachia: circa 1370
> Romania: 1385
> Hungary: 1417
> Germany: 1417
> Switzerland: 1418
> France: 1419
> Denmark: 1420
> Italy: 1422

---

*Their language belongs to the Indo-Aryan branch of Indo-European and shares many similarities with the idioms of Kafiristan (now the Nuristan Province in northeastern Afghanistan), and the tribes of the Hindu Kush.

Bologna: 1422

Catalonia: 1447

Spain: 1447

England: 1460

Scotland: 1492

Russia: 1500

Poland: 1501

Sweden: 1512

Finland: end of the sixteenth century

A variety of legends explain why the Gypsies have no nation and are condemned to wander eternally.[6] In Bulgaria it is said that this nomadic behavior is due to the curse cast by Moses against the pharaoh, the King of the Gypsies.[7]

It is their name, however, that feeds the myth of their Egyptian origin. In France they were initially called *Égyptiens* (Egyptians) and later *Bohémiens* (Bohemians), *Manouches,* and *Romanichels.* Similarly, in Greece they are called *Gyphtoi* (γύφτοι), in Albania *Evgit,* in Holland *Egyptnaaren* then *Giptenaers*), in Britain *Egipcions* (and later *Gypsies*), in Spain *Egiptcians* (later *gitanos*); whereas we find terms related to the French word *Tzigane* in countries such as Bulgaria (*Cinganin*), Romania (*Cigánu*), Germany (*Zigeuner*), Norway (*sigøynere*), and Italy (*Zingari, Zingani*). The Gypsies call themselves *Roma* (sg. *Rom;* fem. *Romni*), *Romani/ Romany, Čhave, Sintei, Mánuš* ("man"), and *Kale* or *Mellĕle* ("dark" or "black").

Other names were given to them in Scandoromani (the Romani dialect of Scandinavia): *Romanisœi, Romanoar,* and *Tavringer.*

Many cultural facets of this traditionally oral people—and therefore a culture more susceptible than others to the erosion of time—have vanished since the nineteenth century, which saw the creation of a discipline later called "Gypsology." "We have no right to any form of writing; that is our curse," stated the leader of a Gypsy clan in the 1950s,*[8] and it is said in Bulgaria that the Gypsies are illiterate because a donkey ate the alphabet that God had given to them.[9]

It was in the 1870s that the linguist and folklorist Heinrich Adalbert von Wlislocki (1856–1907)—considered by Charles Godfrey Leland as the first "Gypsologist"[10]—began to take an interest in the Gypsies of Transylvania and the Hungarian Banat region. During the era when Heinrich von Wlislocki was collecting information, their numbers were estimated at 905,000, with the bulk of the population concentrated in Transylvania, where they performed various professions. Some of them were settled in one place and were derisively described as *Gletecor*, "without culture." The others, who remained nomadic, were called *Kontorár*, "those who live under the tent," and were divided into four tribes—Leïla, Kukuya, Ašani, and Tçale—each of which had its own legend of origin and followed the orders of a chief (*šaibidjo*).†

During the summer of 1883, Wlislocki accompanied one of these nomadic tribes, following them for several months as they traveled into southeastern Hungary, and performed the duties of an ethnologist in the field and a folklorist. He collected a wealth of information, and the principal works on this people are always inspired by his research. He systematically gathered rites, traditions, tales and legends, songs, proverbs, nursery rhymes, jokes, magic charms, and healing recipes, which altogether amount to a very rich collection. For Wlislocki, "the most ancient and primitive literary manifestation of a people is in its tales and legends,

---

*Around 1850 they already considered their lack of writing as a curse. Moreover, they even have a legend that explains this absence: they were stripped of their writing for having forged the nails that were used to fasten Jesus to the cross.

†The most significant groups or tribes are called *gákkiyá*, a word coined from *gakko*, meaning "parent, cousin"; the less important are called *máhliyá*, which comes from *máhlo*, "friend."

which reveal its way of thinking, its past and present circumstances, its concepts and customs, and its deepest spirit in the most genuine way." Stating that we could not understand these stories without an extensive, in-depth knowledge of the people to whom they belong, he goes on to remark:

> But how many things that are full of sense and meaning for this people in their tales and legends remain obscure and inexplicable, and often seem trivial or even pointless, to one who is ignorant of the secret and subtle connections, the invisible threads upon which this very sense and meaning depend, just as the connection to the inner life of these people, which is reflected in these tales, also remains unknown.

Without preliminary study, it is impossible "to grasp the inner life and its manifestations without the most exact knowledge of the people itself, without entering completely into its sphere of existence." Wlislocki is therefore pleading for a rectification of the image of the Gypsies.

> Admittedly, people ascribe all sorts of wondrous, impossible, or abominable things to the Gypsies because the unfamiliarity with the mores, practices, customs, and relationships of this group is so great that one may conceivably say just about anything without being held accountable—but it should also not be forgotten that the Gypsies especially have quite a few convicts and reckless and disheveled characters among them.[11]

And Wlislocki underscores the distinguishing features of the Gypsy soul: "the profound understanding of nature, both animate and inanimate—the intimacy with nature's transformations and the love for it as the mother of all."[12]

Wlislocki decided to share daily life with the Gypsies,

practicing an *avant la lettre* form of "participatory ethnology" during an era when the Gypsy folklore of Transylvania was at its zenith.[13]

> In the summer of 1883, I decided to draw my information directly from a genuine source, collecting it from from a group of Transylvanian nomads rather than from the sedentary Gypsies. I lived with them for several months and accompanied them through the whole of Transylvania and southeastern part of Hungary. During this time, in addition to many other extremely interesting particulars, I have gathered together the tales and legends I am publishing here by following one fundamental principle: without worrying about the value of the source, every text I have reproduced here was told to me by at least two individuals and recognized as forming part of the Gypsy heritage. In other words, I have heard each story told by two people at different times and in different places, and I copied them down literally. Of two variants, I have always chosen to include the more beautiful and interesting version. In order to ensure the commercial success of this collection, it was necessary to leave out the original Romani texts.[14]

Other researchers imitated Wlislocki, such as the magistrate Richard Liebich in 1863. In 1868 the Earl of Mitrović, Rudolf Wratislaw, provided a description of the life, origin, and language of the Austrian Gypsies; Francis H. Groome (1851–1902) published a collection of folktales in 1899; the traveler and geographer Anton von Etzel (1821–1870) supplied us with information on the Norwegian Gypsies; Josef Ješina published a grammar and dictionary of the Gypsy language in the 1880s,[15] completing the labors of Wlislocki; the Slovene linguist Franz Xavier Miklošič (1813–1891) pursued his interest in the migrations of this people in Europe; and, in 1915, F. M. Pabanó wrote a history of the Spanish Gitanos.

More recently the Dominican Joseph Chatard transcribed the testimony of Zanko, the leader of the Kalderash tribe; this was followed in 1953 by the work of Jules Bloch (1880–1953),[16] a Sanskrit specialist; in 1973 by the studies of Françoise Cozannet; and in 1991 by Veronika Görög-Karady's investigation. In parallel to these books, journals came into existence including that of the Gypsy Lore Society in England, the *Journal of the Gypsy Lore Society,* which was renamed *Romani Studies* in 2000; in France the *Études tsiganes* (Gypsy Studies) has been issued since 1995; and in Germany there has been the *Gießener Hefte für Tsiganologie* (Giessen Notebooks on Gypsology) published from 1984–1986, followed by the *Tsiganologische Studien* (Gypsology Studies) from 1990–1992. It should also be noted that the universities of Leipzig and Prague possess a Gypsology department and that the Bulgarian Academy of Science has been publishing the *Studii Romani* since 1991. In France one publishing house, Wallâda, has dedicated itself to introducing this culture for more than twenty years.[17]

Mythology has remained the poor stepsister, so to speak, among Gypsology studies. To the best of my knowledge only the attempt at a systematic survey by Hermann Berger, which was part of a larger anthology published in 1984, has laid the foundations for further research. It must be said that the task is formidable, since no past scholar of mythology has ever committed the myths of this people to paper. To rediscover them we must use the method of Jacob Grimm[18] or, more recently, that of Aldor J. Greimas,[19] which closely examine and analyze the tales, legends, and testimonies that have been collected concerning Gypsy rites and traditions. Since these are peoples of an oral culture, credit is due to the collectors of folk traditions and ethnologists who assembled the materials from which it is possible to form some idea of the mythology of the Gypsies.

In Gypsy mythology, as in many other mythologies around the world, the elements, the natural phenomena, the celestial bodies have been anthropomorphized and awarded the title of "king." We have the "Wind King," the "Sun King," the "King of the Mist," and so forth. Originally the word *god* designated to the Gypsies everything that was above the Earth such as the sun, the sky, and the clouds; and then, under the influence of Christianity, it refers to the God of the Christians, who is seen as the creator of the world but only an indirect creator of human beings—who they believe were born from a tree. The religious concepts of the Roma testify to a profound syncretism of pagan and Christian elements. Having coexisted with numerous peoples of different religions over the course of their tribulations, the Gypsies have certainly borrowed elements from them, but they nevertheless maintained an old pagan reservoir of beliefs that reveals its existence in the worship of nature, stars, and elements. Those Gypsies who adopted Christianity revised the Gospels, and those of the Muslim countries have likewise borrowed certain figures. This was all still evident in the nineteenth century, but since then, with many things being forgotten, it is all the more important to gather together the old testimonies.

For their part, animals are often human beings that have been metamorphosed because of a misdeed, which cannot fail to bring Ovid's *Metamorphoses* to mind. For example, the cuckoo was formerly a rich peasant who threw Saint Nicholas outside because he had eaten his bread and drunk his wine. But humans and animals also share a close bond, and the spirit of an animal can travel in to the body of a man.

Three major motifs make up the common core of beliefs that is reflected in the myths and legends of the Gypsies. These are the *mountain,* which was regarded as sacred and was worshipped; the *forest;* and the *waters.* These motifs are ubiquitous, and it is in these locations that supernatural creatures and gods reside.

The world is full of spirits who have an effect on humans and animals; they can furnish all kinds of knowledge, reveal what is hidden, and make it possible to see what remains hidden to the majority of people. These spirits include the spirits of nature as well as those of humans, living and dead.

Nature is indeed inhabited by supernatural beings, fairies who are led by a queen, undines, ogres, giants, dog-people, and so forth. There are demons—often zoomorphic and most frequently appearing in the form of a worm—who attack human beings by sending them illnesses, and there is, of course, the devil, who has lost his mythic nature. He is now a man whose specific nature is revealed by physical details—for example, small horns poking out from beneath his headgear or goose feet—or by the kinds of clothing he wears. This figure has obviously often supplanted other kinds of fantastic beings.

The origin myths, which appear in the form of etiological legends, form the ancestral memory of the tribes, and they are often better preserved in Eastern and Central Europe than elsewhere. These legends are closely related to the daily life of the Gypsies. One legend explains the origin of the people and the reasons for the tribulations they suffer, another explains their appearance, a third explains the history of the great flood, and so forth. Because, over time, they forgot their ancient origins in India, this people created the myth of their Egyptian origin and provided themselves with ancestral legends. One of these legends maintains that the different tribes descended from men whom a witch had transformed into dogs. The origin myth of the Leïla people states that the tribe emerged from the hair of a fairy, while the origin myth of the Kukuyá claims that they were born from the union of a young Bohemian and a chthonic spirit known as a *pçuvuši*.

A number of these myths offers a consolation and a form of compensation with the logic that "if it is this way, it is because . . ." This created the necessary conditions for the emergence of a *Weltanschauung* that one finds among many different peoples of the world: evils are due to a transgression or sacrilege that is punished, for example, by the end of the Golden Age, which was destroyed by a great flood, or by the loss of everything that makes a nation.*

TRANSCRIPTIONS AND PRONUNCIATION

There are around fifteen different Gypsy languages, and the transcription and names will vary depending on the ethnologist or folklorist who collected them. Furthermore, the language has been expanded by words from all the different nationalities with whom the Roma have had relationships. There should be surprise, then, that different spellings will sometimes be found for the same term in this dictionary as it is my intent to faithfully transcribe everything as it appears in the source texts.

C, ç: *ts*

t': as in "tea"

Č: *tch*

H, ḥ: [x]

l': silent as in the Spanish *"caballero"* or the French *"feuille"*

Š, š: *sh* as in "shawl"

u: as in "you"

Ž, ž: as in "measure"

d': as in "dignity"

ň, ñ: as in the French word *"digne"*

SYMBOLS

✦ refers to another entry

📖 sources and bibliography

---

*"We no longer have any power, nor a land, nor a nation, nor a chieftain, nor a church, nor any writing . . . for they have been drowned in the sea forever."[20]

Note: References to Wlislocki, *Volkglaube,* are to his *Volksglaube und religiöser Brauch der Zigeuner* (1891) rather than to his later work on the Magyars that bears a similar title.

ABBREVIATIONS

fem. feminine   **masc.** masculine

pl. plural   **sg.** singular

NOTES

1. Cf. Bordigoni, *Gitans, Tsiganes, Roms,* and the quite revelatory collective anthology edited by Uerlings and Parut, *Zigeuner und Nation.*
2. Cf. Heister, *Ethnographische und geschichtliche Notizen über die Zigeuner,* 98–107.
3. Thomasius, *Dissertatio philosophica de cingaris.*
4. Vaillant, *Grammaire, Dialogues et Vocabulaire de la Langue des Bohémiens ou Cigains,* 88–89. For a particularly negative contemporary portrait of the *modorani,* cf. Stoichita, *Fabricants d'émotion,* 35.
5. See also Parut, "Wlislocki's Transylvanian 'Gypsies' and the discourses on Aryanism around 1900."
6. Cf. Druts and Gessler, *Skazki i pesni tsygan Rossii,* 213–14.
7. Cf. Kenrick and Golemanov, "Three Gypsy Tales from the Balkans," 59–60.
8. *Zanko, chef tribal chez les Chalderash,* 13.
9. Nounev, "Legends," 48–61.
10. "Dr. Heinrich v. Wlislocki, who is probably more practically familiar with this Gypsy life and language in every form than any scholar who ever lived" (*Journal of the Gypsy Lore Society* 1 [1889], 106).
11. Wlislocki, *Märchen und Sagen der transsilvanischen Zigeuner,* v, vii, viii.
12. Wlislocki, *Märchen und Sagen,* xiv.
13. Görög-Karady, ed. *Contes d'un Tzigane hongrois,* 16.
14. Wlislocki, *Märchen und Sagen,* xv.

15. Ješina, *Slovnik česko-cikánský a cikánsko český, jakož i cikánsko-české pohádky a povídky,* published in Kutná Hora in 1889, which includes a collection of Gypsy folktales and fables.

16. Bloch, *Les Tsiganes.*

17. Cf. Mingot-Tauran, "Éditer la parole tzigane. L'expérience de Wallâda."

18. Grimm, *Deutsche Mythologie.*

19. Greimas, *Of Gods and Men.*

20. *Zanko,* 31.

DICTIONARY OF
GYPSY MYTHOLOGY

ADAM and EVE (Damo and Yehwah): ✦ Anthropogeny, Gypsy, Rom.

ALAKO: This myth is only known among the Norwegian Gypsies. At the time the Gypsies came to Assas, in their land of Assaria, the great God (*baro devel*) sent his son Dundra to the Earth in the form of a man so that he could reveal the secret law to them and they could write it down in a book. Once this had been done, Dundra left the Earth and returned to his kingdom, the moon, which has since then been called Alako (a name that is reminiscent of the Finnish word *alakku,* "waning moon"). His enemies, the Christians and the Turks, attempt ceaselessly to drive him away from the moon, and it is at these times that the moon wanes. But when Dundra strikes with his sword and spear the horns of the new moon appear and grow until they become the full moon. It is at this time that the Gypsies kneel down between the trees of the forest and give praise to the victorious god who will one day help them to defeat the Turks and regain the land from which this people have chased them.

Dundra brings the souls of the dead to his kingdom. His enemies are the Christians, the Turks, the devil (*Beṅg*), and the Christ (*Gern*). He is depicted as a man standing upright holding a feather in his right hand and a sword in his left, and this image is in the safekeeping of the chieftain of the tribe. The weddings of new couples are consecrated in the presence of this image.

✦ *Beṅg, Dundra*

📖 Etzel, *Vagabondenthum und Wanderleben in Norwegen*, 40–43; Berger, "Mythologie der Zigeuner," 787.

ANA: This is the queen of the fairies (*kešalyia*). She takes her name from the way she acts: she will indeed shout *Ana!* ("Bring it!") to every man she sees who has gotten lost on the mountain. The person who hears this command must quickly hunt for a frog or an insect and cast it into the nearest bush, or else he should flee because Ana will smash his head with a rock. But whoever heeds her call and obeys it will receive a small flask from her filled with a certain kind of water that imparts enormous strength. She dwells alone in her black palace high up in the mountains. She leaves it from time to time in the form of a frog.

She married the king of the *loçolicos*. To sleep with her he had to put her to sleep by making her eat a magpie brain. From him she gave birth to the demons of illnesses. When the ninth one was born, her husband, horrified at how hideous it looked, agreed to leave his wife on condition that she would abandon to his subjects each *kešalyi* that was ninety-nine years old.

The staff of the Gypsies is triangular in shape and has one word on each of its three faces. Together they form the phrase "Help us, Ana."

✦ *Kešalyia, Loçolico, Magpie*

📖 Wlislocki, *Aus dem inneren Leben*, 3–4, 178; Wlislocki, *Volksglaube*, 22.

ANT (*handja, kirja*): There is a Gypsy folktale that tells how an ant saved from drowning by a young man gave his rescuer one of his eggs and recommended to break it whenever he needed help. When the boy followed this advice, an army of ants emerged and

Ana, queen of the fairies, gave
birth to the demons of illnesses.

accomplished the task that he had been ordered to complete. In
another tale the King of the Ants, a hybrid being that is half man
and half insect, gives one hair from his head to a young man who
had removed a bee stinger stuck in his jaw and tells him to burn it
when he finds himself in danger.

📖 Wlislocki, *Volksdichtungen,* no. 44; *Märchen und Sagen,* no. 47.

ANTHROPOGENY: When God planted his staff in the pri-
mordial ocean, a large tree sprouted up and the first human beings
fell from its branches or leaves.

Another tradition says that at the command of God, the devil
crafted two statuettes (*popusha*) of a man and a woman from soil
he brought up from the bottom of the sea, but he was unable to
make them speak. God, the Pouro Del (*pouro* meaning "old" and
del meaning "God), laid his hands upon the statuettes. Two trees
immediately sprang forth from the ground, one behind the man
and the other behind the woman, surrounding them with their
branches and transforming them into flesh and giving them life.
This is how Damo (Adam) and Yehwah (Eve) were born. Then

God commanded one of the trees to bear apples and the other to bear pears and told Yehwah to eat apples and Damo to eat pears.

When God went forth to see what had become of the human beings, he encountered three at the side of the road, who were waiting to be given names. He named the first one Gorgio, and that individual became rich. It should be noted that this name designates those who are not Gypsies, the *Gadje* (sg. *Gadjo*). Because the second one was black, God gave him the name of "Negro," and he was too lazy to work unless he was forced to. The third was brown and peacefully smoked his pipe. When God dubbed him with the name "Rom," this individual stood up and thanked him. Charles G. Leland notes that the word *Rom* is related to the Sanskrit *remna,* a verb meaning "to wander, to lurk." Therefore, according to this etiological legend, the Roma are wanderers.

According to another tradition, God took some flour and water, shaped some small humans from it, and placed them in the oven. His first attempt created black men, because the dough was overcooked; his second attempt resulted in the white people, because he did not leave them in long enough. The third time was the charm, and the perfectly cooked dough produced the Roma with their pretty tan color.

Other legends inform us that in very ancient times God would resurrect those who died one year after their death. But on seeing how two sisters would only kiss their brother, just restored to life, through a handkerchief because of their disgust, he became irritated and stopped reviving the dead.

📖 Ros', *Voyage maison,* 77–78; Leland, *The English Gypsies,* 319; Kabakova, *Contes et Légendes tsiganes,* 21; Rehfisch, *Gypsies, Tinkers and Other Travellers,* 145.

APPLE (*pchabaj, phabay, phabuyépia, pomya*): Apples, often golden apples, play a very important role in the traditions of the Gypsies. They can provide immortality, fertility, and restore life.

In some narratives the tree that bears this fruit has become sterile because a serpent is gnawing on its roots. The tree is guarded by nine dogs, and a white blanket that grants invisibility hangs from one of its branches; a person who drapes this blanket over himself will therefore be able to pick its apples. Sometimes there is a fairy who changes anyone who steals the fruit of this tree into a dog. The spirits of the water (*nivaši*) often demand apples that people offer them so as to gain their good will.

In front of the house of King Mist, one of the sons of Earth (Pçuv), there stands a tree that bears three golden apples guarded by dog-men. The first apple will give people riches, the second will give them happiness, and the third provides permanent good health.

There are other apples that plunge the one who eats them into a deep slumber. A dead domestic snake that has been buried in the garden gives birth to a tree bearing golden apples.

One of the frequent tasks imposed on a hero seeking to marry a princess is to bring back to her father the three golden apples that grow on the Tree of All Seeds. Thanks to a marvelous horse—*maschurdalo* in metamorphosed form—who gives him advice, he manages to slay the gigantic serpent (dragon) that holds the crown of the tree in its mouth.

◆ *King Mist, Maschurdalo, Nivaši, Tree of All Seeds*

📖 Wlislocki, *Volksdichtungen*, no. 20; *Märchen und Sagen*, nos. 10, 15, 16, 24, 48; Groome, *Gypsy Folk-Tales*, 29, 36, 40, 57, 65–66.

ARMIKO: When Armiko was born the Ursitory determined that he would only live for the length of time it took for a branch to be consumed in the fire. The child's grandmother pulled it out of the fireplace and gave it to his mother. The Ursitory were fooled, and the child lived a good, long life.

The theme of a connection between life and the combustion of an object can be found at an earlier time in classical antiquity (the legend of Meleager) and in the Scandinavian literature of the

Middle Ages with the story of the candle owned by the Norse hero Norna-Gest.

✦ *Ursitory*

📖 Ros', *Voyage maison*, 28.

AŠANI, ASHANI: This is the name of a Romanian tribe of Transylvanian Gypsies whose origin is explained by the following legend. The husband of a childless couple was sleeping one day beneath a tree and dreamed that a *chagrin* told him to kill a cow, burn its meat to ashes and give them to his wife to eat, and then to sleep with her on the hide of the cow. The man heeded all these instructions and, nine months later, his wife gave birth to a little girl who burst out laughing when she was born, which caused her parents to give her the name of Ašani, "the laughing one." She married, had children of her own, and laughed all the time—even on the day when her husband broke his leg. He flew into a rage and drove her away with all her children.

✦ *Chagrin*

📖 Wlislocki, *Vom wandernden Zigeunervolke*, 72–73.

AVALI: ✦ Will-o'-the-Wisp

BAT (*bachtáli*): When he was still young, the king of the devils (*legbarer beṅg*, "the high devil") loved women and would kiss them while they were sleeping. His grandmother became angry at his behavior. She ate a mouse and then daubed her grandson's lips with her own turds. The next time he kissed a woman on the lips this brought about the birth of the first bat.

When someone who is betrothed spots a bat she should spit, for it is believed that her saliva will fall, burning hot as pitch, on the tongues of all people who are looking at her marriage with an evil eye. If a bat flutters around the panes of a window or enters a room it means that one of its inhabitants will fall ill or die. The blood of a bat poured on the feathers plucked from a black hen and worn around the neck will heal stiffness there.

   📖 Wlislocki, *Aus dem inneren Leben,* 115.

BAVOLSHI: This is the name of the wind demons.

   ✦ *Pantheon*

BEAR (*urs, bero*): This creature is born from a young girl who became pregnant without having known a man.

   📖 Djordjević, "Erzählungen moslimischer Zigeuner aus dem Moravagebiete in Serbien," 155.

BEŃG, BENGY, BENK: This is the Gypsy name for the devil. The word comes from the Sanskrit word *pangka,* which means "mud." In Indian mythology there is a hell consisting of mud. The word *beńg* is also often used to designate a monster or a dragon.

✦ *Devil*

BIMUYAKRO ("Without Lips"): Heartbroken at being rejected by the beautiful Lolerme with whom he had fallen in love, Bimuyakro paired up with a *nivaši,* whose kiss cost him his lower lip. The water spirit dove into a lake with him and installed him in her home. From then on he lived a very comfortable life. Nine days later his lover told him he would have to leave her for one day and one night, and she brought him back up to solid ground. He rejoined his tribe, where to his surprise he discovered, upon sticking his hand into his pocket, that it was filled with gold coins. The *nivaši* gave birth to a boy who had no bones but was able to speak and run about immediately after being born. She told Bimuyakro that he would bring misfortune to men and that he would not be able to come back to the lake until thirty years had passed. Bimuyakro left the water spirit and married Lolerme, but one day, while he was crossing over a bridge, a young *nivaši* emerged from the river, grabbed him, and carried him below the water where he drowned. This narrative is strongly reminiscent of European folktales about the water spirit known as Melusine, in which marrying a supernatural woman eventually leads to death.

✦ *Nivaši*

📖 Wlislocki, *Märchen und Sagen,* no. 23; Lecouteux, *Mélusine et le Chevalier au Cygne.*

BIRTH (*tarneben*): Women give birth outdoors near running water, never in the tent of the Gypsy caravan. They wash themselves in this water, then plunge their child into it while giving him a secret name that no one should ever use, and which even the child's father does not know. This name is used to fool the demons and the angel of death, who is thus unable to call the young child. It is thought that this name has a totemic function. The godfathers give another name to the newborn, a name reserved for the use of the Gypsy community and which is never used in the presence of *gadjé*.

📖 Ville, *Tziganes*, 99ff.; Berger, "Mythologie der Zigeuner," 822.

BITOSO ("the One Who Fasts"): Bitoso is the sixth child of Ana, the queen of the *kešalyia* and the husband of Šilályi. He is the most innocent of all his brothers and sisters. He resembles a small multiheaded worm and causes headaches, stomachaches, and loss of appetite.

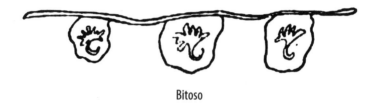

Bitoso

His infants resemble him quite closely, and the illnesses they bring to humanity include toothaches and ringing in the ears. We only know the name of one of them, Serkulo, who causes leg cramps, specifically in the calves.

To treat stomach cramps people would take garlic in brandy, saying the following charm before and after drinking it.

> *O cavore Biteskro,*
> *O cavore miseçeskro,*
> *Amare mamake*
> *Bute hin carñake,*
> *Bute hin siva;*
> *Kiya yoy me prejiav!*

Siva tumenge dav
The mami tumen kamel,
Te nañi mumen marel!

O children of Bitoso,
O children of evil [the demons]
Your grandmother [Ana]
Owns four simples
Owns many heads of garlic;
I will race to her!
I will give you garlic
So that the grandmother will love you
And never beat you again!

✦ *Garlic, Kešalyia, Serkulo, Šilalyi*

📖 Wlislocki, *Aus dem inneren Leben,* 20–23.

BLACK CAT (*kálo mač/murga*): There is a belief that every year black cats will "lay" a sparkling stone that will only remain on Earth for the length of time it takes to count to seven. It then vanishes. With this stone one can open all locked rooms, and it can change metals into gold.

📖 Wlislocki, *Volksdichtungen,* 282.

BLACK HEN: When a cow urinates while it is being milked, Gypsies believe this is a sign it has been bewitched. Some of its urine is collected and mixed with onion peels and the egg of a black hen while reciting a charm.

✦ *Urme*

BLESSED MOUNTAINS (*baçtalo bar*): The elevations of the terrain that bear this name are hollow. They are the dwelling places for men who have been transformed into snakes and women who have been transformed into turtledoves and who guard immense treasures. They are under a curse of King Sun for having profaned these places at one time during their lives. A man will be freed if a young woman falls in love and chooses him for a husband; a woman will be freed if it is a young man who chooses her.

A female dog with four eyes dwells in one or the other of the Blessed Mountains. It is possible to both see and hear her. Treasures gathered by the serpent people can be found there: glossopetrae ("tongue stones") that make it possible to foretell the future.

It is on these mountains where vows are formulated, but it is imperative that the individual does not drink or eat anything except mare's milk for three days and should abstain from all sexual relations. Next, the individual must ascend the mountain before sunrise while carrying a piece of meat, two eggs from a white hen, two apples, and a little animal blood in a bowl. At the moment when the sun appears the individual should eat these foods and swear his oath. Before descending the mountain the shells of the eggs and the bowl must be buried so that witches will not be able to thwart the request. The dirt that one can gather there possesses magical properties; namely, the power to open and close the doors to the Other World.

It will be noted that *baçt* comes from the Persian *bakht* ("fortune, prosperity, happiness"), and what Gypsies say for "Good Day" is "Be Lucky!" (*T'aves baçtalo*).

✦ *Glossopetrae, King Sun*

📖 Wlislocki, *Aus dem inneren Leben*, 60–64, 81.

BLOND MAN: ✦ King Mist

BLUE FLOWER (*vunete luludyi*): This flower grows above buried treasures on the night of Pentecost and casts a bluish light that can be seen from a great distance. When this happens the flower should not be picked; instead, the individual who found it should wait until it retreats back into the ground—only then can he or she dig there to gain the treasure.

📖 Wlislocki, *Vom wandernden Zigeunervolke*, 159; Wlislocki, *Volksglaube*, 157.

BRANDY: ✦ Revenant

BUTYAKENGO ("the Many-eyed One"): According to the nomadic Gypsies of Serbia and Turkey, this is the name of the guardian spirit who lives in every human being. The name is formed from the words *but,* meaning "several," and *yak,* which means "eye." When a dead person goes into the Other World he leaves a part of his soul (*gotri jipneskro*) behind on Earth, and this soul then passes on to his or her descendants. The remaining soul-portion of a father migrates into the eldest son; that of a mother, into the oldest daughter. This would appear to be a type of double

that is quite similar to the *hamr* and *fylgja* found among the ancient Scandinavians that moves from the father to his eldest son, from the mother to the eldest daughter, and from the grandfather to the youngest son of his son. Butyakengo can exit and return to the sleeping body of its owner. It is believed that he resides in the little finger of the left hand, which is called *kekeraška,* "magpie." Using signs he can alert the person of imminent danger. When the person is sick, he will leave him or her until he or she is well again. He exits the body through the right ear and returns back into it via the left ear. He spends the night outside of the body and keeps watch over the individual's property.

📖 Wlislocki, *Aus dem inneren Leben,* 18–19, 64–65; Wlislocki, *Volksglaube,* 43–47; Berger, "Mythologie der Zigeuner," 811; Lecouteux, *Encyclopedia of Norse and Germanic Myth, Magic, and Folklore,* 102 (*fylgja*), 124 (*hamr*); Bonnefoy, ed., *Roman and European Mythologies,* 230.

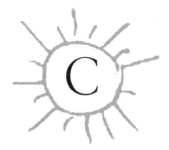

CAÏN: ✦ Pantheon

ČARANA/TSCHARANA: This is a gigantic bird that lives for 999 years before dying, unless it suckles on the breast of one single woman every night. It lives in an iron castle on top of a mountain, where it holds prisoner the Urme that suckles it. It is charged with the duty of preventing the King of the Moon from having too many children—the stars—and every month it pecks away a good part of his face and body. The Čarana are the servants of Matuyá, the queen of the fairies (Urme). These servants have built a castle for her, where a black hen is locked in an iron cabinet protecting the life of the bird inside an egg. If someone should ever make off with this egg, the Čarana will die. If the Čarana dies from some other cause, the hen will come out of the cabinet and secretly lay a small egg in the womb of a woman who, after seven days of hard suffering, will give birth to a little Čarana without realizing it. A woman who endures this experience will never give birth to anything but dwarfs from that point on. If the Čarana drinks the urine of a female sorceress, it will immediately become a gigantic bird.

There is a celestial body called the "Star of Čarana" and the "Star of the Father"—names that must refer back to a myth that is now forgotten. This star appears at the onset of spring, but it has not been identified. It is likely to be Regulus, which together with Arcturus and Spica form the asterism called the "Spring Triangle."

When a pregnant woman grows too large, people commonly say that "she is carrying the egg of the Čarana" (*hin lake yandro Tsharaneskro*).

✦ *King of the Moon, Matuyá, Urme*

📖 Wlislocki, *Volksdichtungen*, 239, 274–78; Wlislocki, *Aus dem inneren Leben*, 67–68; Wlislocki, *Volksglaube*, 8–9; Wlislocki, *Märchen und Sagen*, 21–24, 121; Ficowski, *Le Rameau de l'arbre*, 154.

ČARAYA: This star, which is still called "Star of the Father," marks the arrival of spring.

📖 Wlislocki, *Märchen und Sagen*, no. 55.

CERESROBARA: This is the name that is given to the "thunder-bolts" or "thunder stones" (*ceraunia*) that can be found in the mountains. They possess a secret healing property for the heart and body (*trupos te vodyi*), a virtue that is extended to the plants growing in the nearby proximity. The Bulgarian and Serbian Gypsies call them glossopetrae (tongue stones—*bicibakro bar*) and use them for advice on what actions they should take. They smear one of these stones with animal fat and then bury it beneath a stretch of grass and dirt. They then water this "hill." If the fat is still there the next day, the individual should go ahead with what they had planned to do.

📖 Wlislocki, *Aus dem inneren Leben*, 52.

CHAGRIN, CHAGRINO, HÁGRIN: This is the name of the personification of a disease. The *chagrin* takes the form of a yellow porcupine that is around twenty inches long and one span wide. It attacks horses during the night, especially female horses that have just given birth. The *chagrin* rides its victims until they are covered with sweat. It also snarls up their manes and exhausts them. To prevent it from coming near the animals a gruel is brewed from horse hairs, a little salt, bat's blood, and some flour, which is then smeared over the horse's hooves. Once the dish that held the gruel is empty it must be hidden within a hollow tree. Another remedy involves tying the horse to a stake that has been smeared with garlic juice and a circle made all around it with red thread while speaking a conjuration that commands the *chagrin* to jump into a brook and drown (*Sáve miseç ač káthe, / Ác ándre lunge táve, / Andre leg páshader páñi. / De tu tire páñi / Andre çuča cháriñeyá, / Andre tu sik mudárá!*). On Christmas night the ashes of a branch from an ash tree are spread beneath the horses to prevent the *chagrin* from torment-ing them. Another good form of protection is to hang or nail a weasel skin in the proximity of the horse or horses.

The claws of the *chagrin* have the reputation of increasing sexual prowess, and if you rub the body of a dead person with the ashes of the middle claw from its right foot you can restore him or her to life.

According to Hermann Berger, *ḫágrin* could come from the Sanskrit word *kantakarana,* from which the Punjabi word *kādērnā,* "porcupine," also derives.

✦ *Weasel*

📖 Wlislocki, *Volksdichtungen,* no. 5, no. 32; Wlislocki, *Vom wandernden Zigeunervolke,* 72, 144, 210; Wlislocki, *Volksglaube,* 136; Leland, *Gypsy Sor-cery and Fortune Telling,* 91–94; Berger, "Mythologie der Zigeuner," 793.

CHANGE OF SEX: This was the punishment meted out by one of the King of the Moon's daughters to a young musician who unintentionally caused the death of her sister. This motif was most likely borrowed from a Greek tale during the time of the tribula-tions of the Gypsies, for the stories are practically identical, except for some differences due to local variation. According to Hahn, the basis for the depiction of the change of sex lies with the different phases of the moon: in Hindu mythology the son of Manu first appeared as a man (the full moon) and then as a woman (the last quarter). From that time on, Manu appeared alternatively as a man or woman each month. This change of sex is reminiscent of the story concerning the prophet Tiresias. His staff disturbed two snakes that were mating, and he was transformed into a woman. He remained in this guise for seven years. During the eighth year he again came across the same mating serpents. He struck them a second time with his staff and was turned back into a man (Ovid, *Metamorphoses,* III, 316–38). The origin of all these legends would seem to be India, particularly the story of Ida, the daughter of Manu. She was changed into a man by Mitra and Varuna, and then back into a woman by Shiva.

✦ *King of the Moon*

📖 Wlislocki, *Volksdichtungen,* no. 34; Hahn, *Griechische und albanesische Märchen,* no. 58; Benfey, *Pantschatantra,* 42–45.

CHRISTMAS (*Kolonda, božila jevende, Mul divvus*): The week that precedes Christmas is called the "great week" (*baro burko*) and is a time when remedies and amulets are crafted. The blood of a bat that is killed at this time will heal men and beasts who suffer from bloating.

On Christmas Eve the *múlo* come out and are on the watch for women. It is therefore necessary to place a handkerchief with a little camphor or a nutmeg in front of their cave. On Christmas night the animals speak, but one must not spy on them; otherwise the fairies (Urma) that visit the beasts and bless them will slay the watcher. If one spreads cinders of the ash tree beneath the horses they will be protected for the entire year against the demon known as *ḫágrin (chagrin)*. It is on this night that it is possible to see the Tree of All Seeds.

✦ *Chagrin, Múlo, Tree of All Seeds, Urme*

📖 Wlislocki, *Vom wandernden Zigeunervolke,* 143–44.

ČIGNO DEVEL ("Little God"): This is the son of Sinpetra (God the Father) and Mary, one of the three sisters who all bear the same name and live in Port Saïd. When Sinpetra saw that three doves were constantly circling Mary's head, he asked her three times if she was ready to receive his breath (*duko*). She accepted and became pregnant. With the assistance of her second sister she gave birth in a stable. At the same time, a star appeared in the sky, the reflection, emanation, heart, and sign of the newborn, "and not only his sign but an actual piece of him," according to Zanko, the chief of the Chaderash. This story, which some scholars believe has its source in the *Infancy Gospel of James,* forms part of what is referred to as "The Gospel of the Gypsies."

✦ *Sinpetra*

📖 *Zanko, chef tribal chez les Chalderash,* IV, 1–49; Berger, "Mythologie der Zigeuner," 821.

ČIGNOMANUŠ: This figure is a dwarf, as his name indicates: it has been coined from *čigno,* "small," and *mánuš,* "man" (cf. Sanskrit *mánusya*). He sometimes possesses the strength of three giants, lives in holes in the ground (like the Germanic *Erdmännlein*) or in a cavern, and gives his obedience to a king. He is kind to orphans and to people suffering from grief, and he often helps them to acquire riches. It is necessary to trim his fingernails, beard, and hair and keep all of them in a handkerchief; by doing so one will find good fortune. He will give riches to anyone who can solve his riddles, but a person who fails to solve them must work for him as his valet.

He chooses to live with an individual and takes care of their livestock, demanding in return a bowl of milk. If the person neglects him or vexes him, he will take off and carry with him the wealth and good fortune of the household.

In one Gypsy fairy tale a hero rescues a dwarf being pursued by a wicked fairy who has taken the form of a frog (*jámbá*). The dwarf brings his rescuer into a cave with several rooms, one of iron, one of silver, and one of gold. This is the home of the king of the dwarfs, who gives him a hair from his beard while saying, "Whenever you find yourself in great danger, and only when you find yourself in great danger—blow on this hair and I will come to your rescue together with my people." Then he gave him some water that transformed anything that touched it into gold, and a rifle that always hit its mark.

✦ *Frog*

📖 Wlislocki, *Volksdichtungen*, 252–55; Wlislocki, *Volksglaube*, 27–28; Wlislocki, *Märchen und Sagen*, nos. 13, 32; Ficowski, *Le Rameau de l'arbre*, 158.

CLOUD (*čmura, volka, felkhoeschnodi*): The clouds are primarily the daughters of King Mist, but they can also sometimes be the victims of an evil spell.

✦ *King Mist*

📖 Wlislocki, *Aus dem inneren Leben*, 50; Wlislocki, *Märchen und Sagen*, 98.

COD: A group of handsome young men were bathing in the sea when along came some women and maidens who asked the men to come out of the water and kiss them. The shy young men swam farther out, and when the young women dove in to join them they all drowned. The lads were changed into codfish.

📖 Leland, *The English Gipsies and Their Language*, Gudlo XXXV.

ČOḪANO, CÏOHANÓ, ČOVAHANO (masc.), ČOVAḪANI (fem.): This word is a derivative of *čovah,* a verb meaning to "bewitch, to perform magic." This word is used by the Gypsies of the Balkans to designate the vampire, meaning the spirit of the dead person that has returned to inhabit its corpse. There is no clear distinction made between it and the *múlo*. The *cĭohano* corresponds to the *tchovekhano* of the Turkish Roma.

A Gypsy woman who has just given birth will burn the placenta of her newborn to prevent the Urma from stealing it and using it to create a vampire that will persecute and torture the child.

✦ *Múlo, Urme*

📖 Berger, "Mythologie der Zigeuner," 790; Vukanović, "The Vampire in Belief and Customs of the Gypsies in the Province of Kosovo-Metohija, Stari Ras and Novopazarski Sandžak, Yugoslavia"; Wlislocki, *Vom wandernden Zigeunervolke,* 92; Groome, *Gypsy Folk-Tales,* 14–18.

COMET: A comet is considered one of the offspring of the King of the Moon (the stars are believed to be the Moon King's children). When there are too many stars in his home and space is lacking, he will hurl one to Earth, where it dies immediately and transforms into small seashells (*cereskeri,* a word coined from *čero,* "sky," and *ker,* "house").

✦ *King of the Moon*

📖 Wlislocki, *Aus dem inneren Leben,* 67.

CRĂCIUN: ✦ Cretchuno

CRETCHUNO: He is the husband of the second Mary, the godmother of the "little God," the son of God (Jesus). He touched the newborn immediately on his birth, thus making him impure, and his wife, in a fury, cut off his hands. But he touched the child one more time, and his hands grew back. This motif is reminiscent of what happened to Salome in the *Infancy Gospel of James* (chapter 4). In this story Salome wishes to learn what Mary's condition is. Her hand is consumed and falls off. An angel commands her to take the hand to the little child and to carry him, and she is cured.

We find a variation of this legend in Romanian traditions, where Cretchuno corresponds to Crăciun, "Christmas." Crăciun was a cruel shepherd who had three daughters, whom he mutilated, and a wife named Crăciuneasa, whom he forbade from performing her vocation as a midwife as well as from offering refuge to strangers. Because she provided lodging to Mary and helped her give birth, he cut off her forearm, which then grew back when the injured area touched the swaddling clothes of Jesus, or else the water of his first bath.

📖 Taloş, *Gândirea magico-religioasă la români,* 100; Jangil, *Voyage maison,* 79.

CROSS (*trušŭl*): This is one of the astral symbols that is depicted on the ceremonial staff belonging to the leader of a Gypsy tribe. In nineteenth-century Norway the Roma were called Stavkarle, "Men of the Staff."

📖 *Zanko, chef tribal chez les Chalderash,* 93–94; Wittich, *Blicke in das Leben der Zigeuner,* 58; Berger, "Mythologie der Zigeuner," 800.

CROW, RAVEN (*korúka*): In Gypsy tales this bird is a human being who has been metamorphosed into this shape by a wicked fairy. If a person blows three times on a feather that has been plucked from its wing, he or she will be able to fly through the air. *Korúka/koràko* comes from the Greek *kōraks* (κόραξ) and rep-

resents a word borrowed by the Roma from another people with whom they coexisted.

  📖 Wlislocki, *Märchen und Sagen,* no. 16.

CUCKOO (*kukuk, koring čiriclo*): A rich peasant once tossed Saint Nicholas out of his house because he had eaten his bread and drunk his wine while the man was away. The saint cursed him to turn into a cuckoo and remain without shelter for his entire life.

    The Roma regard the cuckoo as the bird of the *kešalyia.* If a person offends them in any way they will send a cuckoo to burn down their house. The Gypsies of England respect the cuckoo, for they view it as the soul of a Bohemian trying to reincarnate.

    Anyone who finds a cuckoo's egg on Pentecost or Easter will succeed in all of their undertakings over the course of the year. But anyone who hears this bird singing for the first time of the year while sitting or lying down will suffer from ill health for that entire year. The nomadic Transylvania Gypsies will then say of this individual: "The cuckoo has called him" (*kakukos leske cingardyas*). They believe that the cuckoo is only in good health in the springtime and is sick for the rest of the year, hence its nickname *ciriclo násválo,* the "sickly bird."

  ✦ *Kešalyia*

  📖 Kabakova and Stroeva, *Contes et Légendes tsiganes,* 127; Wlislocki, *Vom wandernden Zigeunervolke,* 124–25; Wlislocki, *Aus dem inneren Leben,* 166; Wlislocki, *Volksglaube,* 147–48; Schwicker, *Die zigeuner in Ungarn und Siebenbürgen,* 149; Payne, "Some Romani Superstitions," 111.

CURKO: The king Josipo lived in Kucela in the country of the Gypsies. He asked a young man by the name of Curko to rid his lands of a gigantic black ogress with six fangs who was devouring all his subjects. Curko went off in search of her, and on finding her she told him that she would spare him if he could tell her how many hairs were on the monarch's head. The young man succeeded in answering this question, and she next asked him: "How many mountains are there in the world?" Again he came up with the right answer. For her last question the ogress asked him how many fangs she had in her mouth. "Six," he answered. Alas, she now had only five, and she ate him up. Then the devil devoured Josipo, and since that time the Gypsies have no longer had a country.

✦ *Devil*

📖 Herrmann, *Märchen und Lieder der Roma,* 73–75.

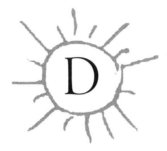

DATURA (*pesoseskro*): This plant (*datura stramonium*) plays a role in one of the origin myths of the Roma. Urged to take a wife and have children who would inherit his wisdom, a man declared he would only marry the woman who promised to obey him. If she disobeyed him, he would curse her. He married and had many children, but one day his wife disobeyed him, and he condemned her to be a plant that humans and animals would avoid, a plant that contained the same number of seeds as she had of children. These children were forced to wander the world while carrying their mother, who had been transformed into a datura plant. The Gypsies are the descendants of this couple. This plant has oracular and medicinal purposes and can bind spirits like the *múlo* and the *nivaši* to one spot. There is a folktale that says: "It is not easy to catch a *nivaši* girl! You have to pretend to be asleep after spreading datura seeds all around you; if a *nivaši* approaches the seeds will bind her to the spot and then you can capture her."

Datura also plays a part in a magical procedure. Stories tell of a woman unable to have children who consulted a wisewoman skilled in magic and was told the following: "Shortly before midnight on Good Friday, go alone to a cemetery where you must dig up the grave of a hanged man and take one of his bones. Bring this bone back home. On Easter Sunday, burn it to ashes. Next you need take the hair of a young girl who is seven years, seven months, seven weeks, and seven days old. Combine this hair with the ashes and boil them together in a pot with datura seeds. Eat this gruel, and you will give birth to a girl."

Men of iron emerged from the datura seeds sowed by a dragon who had spit on them three times.

✦ *Devil, Múlo, Nivaši*

📖 Wlislocki, *Aus dem inneren Leben,* 75; Wlislocki, *Volksdichtungen,* no. 7; Wlislocki, *Märchen und Sagen,* nos. 21, 23, 69; Berger, "Mythologie der Zigeuner," 813.

DAUD ALAYES SALAAM: According to the Gypsies of Bulgaria this was the name of the first smith. He beat the iron with his fist instead of using a hammer and was not burned, until his wife ensured that the opposite happened. Then the heavens sent an anvil to Daud, but the iron was still too hot to be worked. Daud saw a dog that was crossing its forelegs, and the idea came to him for a tongs to pick up the iron without burning his hands. This was how he became the greatest smith the world has ever known.

The Gypsies of Transylvania believe it was the devil who taught men the art of blacksmithing.

📖 Marushiakova and Popov, "Legends," 30–31; Wlislocki, *Aus dem inneren Leben,* 40.

DAY OF THE SHADOWS: ✦ Queen of the Shadows

DEAD (The): The dead who have sinned are transformed in to black crows and must live a long time in this form before they are allowed to enter the Other World. At an earlier time the dead consisted of three distinct groups: the drowned, whose souls belonged to the water spirits who imprisoned them in pots; the murder victims, whose souls traveled into the bodies of wild beasts, where they remained as long as their murderer was still alive and whose soul had not yet passed into an animal where it would remain for centuries before entering the Beyond; and one last group made up of the souls of those who died in their tent (*tan, tanya*) or cabin and who continue to wander the Earth, entering and leaving their bodies at will so long as the latter have not decomposed.

The deceased is washed with salted water then taken out of the tent or the cabin on one of the sides facing the north and not through the entrance. The corpse can also be removed through the window, a practice well known to many other peoples. It is a matter of preventing the dead from coming back. Water is poured into a pail. If it is still there the next day it means that the soul of the deceased has definitely gone back to the Regina Soleika, the queen mother of all the Zingali.

Among the Turkish Gypsies the corpse is sprinkled with the blood of a black hen, and its decapitated body is placed on top of the corpse. If the hen violently beats its wings when its head is chopped off, it is a sign that the dead person is going to find rest in the Beyond (*o múlo arákel pocivipen andre mulengré them*).

The fear of the dead is so intense that Gypsies do not dare speak aloud the name of a dead person while he or she is being cremated or while one is dismantling all that belonged to them. Picking a flower on a grave is seen as a fatal act, one that can attract an incurable disease as expressed by the following verse.

Cignoro hrobosá
Hin shukáres rosá.
Mánge lá pçágávás,
Dos me nákámávás!

On the grave, the rose
Blooms joylessly.
If one seeks to cut me,
It will get its revenge!

The person who sniffs its aroma will lose their sense of smell forever. Insulting a dead person will call down a bloody vengeance.

Vestiges of the worship of the dead can still be observed: No Gypsy will pass by the grave of a person of his clan without pouring several drops of wine, beer, or brandy on it. On the night of January 1 the dead are wished a happy new year and, at midnight, in solemn silence, several drops of an alcoholic drink are poured on the ground. An oath that is sworn over the dead, or which makes reference to them, is inviolable.

The Gypsies believe that white is the favorite color of the dead.

📖 Wlislocki, *Volksdichtungen,* 54, 105–6; Wlislocki, *Märchen und Sagen,* no. 42; Wlislocki, *Vom wandernden Zigeunervolke,* 160, 298–99; Wlislocki, *Volksglaube,* 99; Wlislocki, "Gebräuche der transsilvanischen Zigeuner bei Geburt, Taufe und Leichenbestattung," 267–68; Wittich, *Blicke in das Leben der Zigeuner,* 29; Jangil, *Voyage maison,* 33.

DEATH (*múlo, merrioen, mereben*): A personification of death appears in the tales as a godfather or lover. In the case of the latter, it bears the appearance of a handsome traveler who ends up carrying off the woman he has chosen. When asking who he is, she falls under his power. "Whoever learns this, dies," he answers; but she insists, "I can stand anything, just tell me who you are!" "That is fine, come with me then, I am Death!" The young woman dies on the spot.

✦ *Mountains of the Moon, Múlo*
📖 Wlislocki, *Märchen und Sagen,* 96–97.

DEMONS OF ILLNESSES: These demons are all the spawn of the union of Ana and Loçolico.

✦ *Bitoso, Lili, Lolimišo, Melálo, Minčeskre, Poreskoro, Šilali, Tçaridyi, Tçulo*

DEVIL (*beńg*): Originally the devil (sg. *beńg,* pl. *beńga*) designated a frog, much like Anghra Mainyu in Mazdaism, after which he assumed the form of a snake. In the origin myths and etiological legends he is the ill-fated adversary of God. Whatever form his appearance takes—a handsome young man, a distinguished gentleman, and so forth—he can always be recognized by a certain detail, most often a goose foot or horse hooves. His kingdom is found beneath the ground, at a depth equivalent to ninety-nine days and nights of traveling. The well that leads there has the distinctive feature of closing up on anyone who seeks to go down it, and crushing them. He also lurks in the forests and scares people during the night. He can be put to sleep by spitting three times on the ground and drawing a cross there with your saliva. It is said that he fears women. In the folktales the Gypsies dupe him easily. He grants his help to anyone who eats a plate of beans.

According to Zanko, the leader of the Kalderash, the devil of the Gypsies is not as evil as the devil of the Christians. He is even a companion of God and, like him, born of the Earth (*pçuv, phuv*). He often enters into competition with God, but his opponent always has the upper hand. Zanko also mentions how he lingers in the woods to scare people at night.

The Viennese Gypsies make a distinction between a "good devil" (*lačo beng*), who is close to an angel, and the true one, called the "evil devil" (*nassul, nasdlo beng*).

Sometimes the devil simply takes the place of a fantastical being, such as a fairy or dragon who is responsible for the wealth of siblings but on the condition that the sister never marries. In the tales the sister breaks this prohibition and gives birth to a young goat. This child eats only gold and silver, which he then spits out in a secret hiding place. He cannot reveal anything, as otherwise the devil will transform him into a horse and use him as his steed.

All the devils are subject to the authority of the "supreme devil" (*lagbareder beng*), sometimes referred to as the "king." In turn this devil must obey every command of his grandmother. God created her from a serpent when he spit upon this reptile in disgust. Immediately she gave birth to the supreme devil.

There are sixty-seven "high devils" who are stronger and more powerful than the seven "little devils." All were born in the same way. Every seven thousand years the devil's grandmother gashes her left leg, and each time a demon comes out of the wound.

It should be noted that Satan also has the name of Wafodo guero, "Evil Eye," and that the wind is his sneezing (*Pçurdipen bengeskro báshávipen*).

✦ *Šerkano*

📖 Wlislocki, *Volksdichtungen*, no. 38; Berger, "Mythologie der Zigeuner," 814–15; Ville, *Tziganes*, 115; Kabakova and Stroeva, *Contes et Légendes tsiganes*, 172–74; Görög-Karady, "Problèmes d'identité et récits," 192–93; Ficowski, *Le Rameau de l'arbre*, 72, 227–34; Zanko, *chef tribal chez les Chalderash*, 22–23; Bloch, *Les Tsiganes*, 85; Liebich, *Die Zigeuner*, 32.

DISMEMBERMENT: The cutting of bodies into pieces is a recurring theme of Gypsy narratives and usually appears in a context of resurrection or metamorphosis. In one tale a wicked fairy asks a young man to cut her into pieces and place them into a stewpot so that she could come back out of it as the most beautiful woman in the world. However, he threw all of them into a fountain, thus causing her to die once and for all. Similarly, among the Hungarian Gypsies we find a story in which a fairy dismembers a child, throws all the pieces into a basin, covers it, and then resuscitates the young man using a magic spell. This seems to combine shamanic elements and is also reminiscent of the Cauldron of Immortality, which was highly prized in Celtic mythology. The same process works for animals. A holy man cuts a stork into pieces then casts them into the fire. Once they have been reduced to ash the stork comes back to life, which brings to mind the legend of the phoenix. Moreover, the resurrected stork now possesses a golden feather beneath its left wing, which grows back whenever it has been plucked out. This feather has the property of transforming anything it touches into gold.

Another tale features a five-headed man who heals deaf and blind children by dismembering the youngest one and then throwing the pieces out the window. An instant later, the little child stands up unharmed in the street.

📖 Wlislocki, *Märchen und Sagen*, no. 12, no. 50; Görög-Karady, *Miklós Fils-de-Jument*, 179–81; Groome, *Gypsy Folk-Tales*, 33, 94, 247.

DOG-MAN (*ǰuklanuš*): The three golden apples owned by King Mist are guarded by dog-men. They have the head and "feet" of dogs, they have tongues of iron, and when they howl or moan they cause the mountains to explode. To obtain the apples a would-be thief must piss (*páni keráva*) in their eyes to blind them. The dog-man will cast a curse on the thief: "If you have the apples and you are a man, become a woman! If you are a woman, become a man!"

ǰuklanuš

Their name is formed from *juko/ jukel* meaning "dog," and *manuš,* which means "man."

The dog-men are courageous men that have been transformed into demons by wizards or witches. They live in packs in the mountains and are constantly battling the *loḫoličos,* whom they confront at night in the forests. They are benevolent to humans and will often come to their aid, for example by giving them several drops of their blood when they have been wounded. If a person spits on three hairs from their tail, which they have freely allowed their rescuer to rip out, they will come to his or her assistance.

The dog-man knows the location of a spring whose water cures blindness, but he will only give it to a young woman that agrees to marry him. When a maiden does accept his request and kisses him, he will metamorphose into a handsome young man; he had been changed into this form for having attempted to steal the golden apples of a fairy.

One hair from their head will cure all diseases.

✦ *King Mist, Loçoličos*

📖 Wlislocki, *Volksdichtungen,* nos. 33, 258–60.

DRABARIMÓS: This name refers to the Gypsy custom of traveling here and there to tell fortunes in order to earn money or valuables. Legend has it that when God (*Del*) warned the Roma to leave their country because he intended to punish the king of the Gadje (non-Gypsies) and his people, the elders expressed their worries to him that they would have nothing for their journey. God answered that they would get everything they needed if they sent their women out begging for jewelry, clothing, and food among the Gadje.

✦ *Gypsy Diaspora*

DRAGON (ušáp): Rarely described, the dragon lives on the Mountain of Glass in a castle or house of iron. He is charged with guarding the prisoners there, often young girls who have been transformed and sometimes a maiden he has abducted with the intent to marry her. In some cases he will only free his captives if a pit is prepared for him that is ninety-nine leagues deep and filled with gold so he can bathe in it. He has a wicked fairy for a mother and a sister known for her compassion. The sweat of a dragon is blood. He is endowed with great strength that is concentrated in his tail, a motif that has been well known for centuries. After defeating a sorcerer he seized the magical objects that had belonged to his foe: a flask of the elixir of life, a magic mirror, and a flying carpet.

Despite his name, the dragon is quite close to being a human being: he speaks, has feelings, and experiences fear. He sometimes has the features of an ogre, and he possesses the ability to metamorphose into other beings. He commonly makes deals with towns or cities that supply him with a virgin once a year. The word *dragon* conceals a hybrid creature that is half man, half beast, bordering on the supernatural. When his hairs are cut, burned, and ingested they confer the ability to immediately go wherever it is you desire.

📖 Wlislocki, *Märchen und Sagen*, no. 23; Wlislocki, *Volksdichtungen*, no. 47.

DUNDRA: ✦ Alako

DUNEIRA: This is the name of the first world that God (*Del*) caused to emerge from the water.

📖 Jangil, *Voyage maison*, 79.

DWARF: ✦ Čignomanuš

EAGLE (*šašos, órlos, siv, bišoltilo, bischothilo*): The eagle is the bird of the King of the Sun, who gave it the duty of abducting King Mist's daughter. A young one-eyed man helped him in his task, during the course of which the bird changed him into a golden serpent by spitting on him three times.

EARTH (*Phuru Dai, Phu-amari-day* ["**the divine Earth Mother**"], *Pçuv, Phuv*): She can appear as the triple goddess of fate or as the ruling power of the Pantheon over which she reigns with the Father of the Sky. She is the wife of the heavens, personified as Čero, with whom she has had five sons, including the Moon. She is the mother of God, devils, and clouds.

◆ *King Mist, Lightning, Moon, Mythic Cosmography*

EFTA SHELLENGERI (the "**seven whisperers**" or "**seven whistlers**"): These figures are the seven spirits of women who travel through the air at night like birds. What we have here is a Gypsy version of the Wild Hunt. Charles G. Leland collected the following testimony from the Gypsies of England: "An' the Seven Whistlers are seven spirits of ladies who go by the night, through the air, over the heaven, like birds."

49

Leland, *The English Gipsies and Their Language,* Gudlo XVI, 219; Lecouteux, *Phantom Armies of the Night.*

EGG: It is in the egg of a white hen that the type of earth spirit known as a *pçuvuš* keeps his strength. This is a variation of the belief in the external soul. A black hen holds the life of Čarana, and a chicken holds that of Mašurdalo. The egg of the owl contains the worm of good fortune. Burying the egg of a black hen at the four corners of a cabin will give it protection, and water spirits can be placated by offering them eggs and apples.

✦ *Čarana, Cuckoo, Engagement, Lark, Lightning, Mašurdalo, Owl, Pçuvuš, Soul, Worm of Good Fortune*

EGYPTIAN: The myth of the Gypsies' Egyptian origin has been firmly planted in people's mind-sets since the fifteenth century. In his *Cosmographia* (Basel, 1550), Sebastian Munster writes the following:

> The first time the Gypsies were seen was when 1,417 years had been counted since the birth of Christ. They are a base people who are black, wild, and dirty, and who greatly love to steal, especially the women who aid their husbands in this manner. They have an earl and several knights among them. They have with them several letters and seals that the emperor Sigismond and other princes have given them, granting them the right of free passage in the towns and the countryside. They claim their custom of wandering like pilgrims is a penitence imposed upon them and that they originally came from Lower Egypt. But these are fables. It has been learned full well that this foreign people was born of a vagabond disposition; it has no country, travels the land without working and survives on brigandage, lives like dogs, is without religion although it has its children baptized among the Christians. They live carefree,

roaming from land to land and then returning in several years' time. They are divided into numerous groups and vary their itineraries. . . . This is a strange and savage people. They know many languages and are a plague upon the folk of the countryside. . . . Their old women partake in fortune-telling.

It is easy to discern the presence of all the prejudices that have survived in to the modern era in this old document!

📖 *Journal of the Royal Asiatic Society* 16:2 (1856), 285.

ENGAGEMENT: A week before their wedding day brides go at night to the nearest lake or river, where they stick candles in the bank or hang them from a bush. Among the nomadic Gypsies of Transylvania this is seen as an offering intended to ensure the fruitfulness of the marriage. If the wind blows out the candles it is viewed as a bad omen, and the betrothed couple hasten to toss apples and eggs into the water to placate the water spirits. It is believed that the bride or bridegroom whose candle is extinguished first will be the first to die.

If a Bohemian wishes to get married he hangs a red scarf on the tent of the person he has chosen. If she takes the scarf it is a sign that she has accepted his proposal.

Folktales mention another rite used to determine one's future wife. All the young women of marriageable age are made to line

up in the village, and the suitors are assembled at the end of the meadow. Each of them throws an egg at the one who has caught his eye and is obliged to marry whomever the egg hits. In one story one of the eggs thrown this way strikes a frog who is subsequently revealed to be a young woman who had been metamorphosed.

📖 Wlislocki, *Märchen und Sagen,* no. 24; Wlislocki, *Volksdichtungen,* no. 64.

FAIRY: ✦ Urme

FIRE (*yakh*): After they had insulted the great God (*baro devel*) men were cursed to experience cold, wind, and misery. The frozen devils came to mankind in search of fire, and in return for this they taught humans the crafts of sewing and smithing.

According to a charm collected by Charles G. Leland, fire will drive away the evil spirits Pçuvuse and Nivashi and attract the good fairies.

> *Oh yakh, oh yakh pçabuva,*
> *Pçabuva!*
> *Te čavéstár tu trada!*
> *Tu trada!*
> *Pçávushen te Nivashen*
> *Tire tçuva the traden!*
> *Lače Urmen ávená,*
> *Čaves báçtáles dena.*
> *Káthe hin yov báçtáles,*
> *Andre lime báçtáles!*
> *Motura te ráná,*
> *Te átunci but' ráná,*

Matura te ráná,
Te átunci but' ráná,
Me dav' andre yákherá!
Oh yákh, oh yákh pçabuva!
Rovel čavo: áshuna!

O fire, O fire, burn,
Burn!
Move away from the child!
Go away!
Pçuvuse and Nivashi
Remove your smoke!
Let the good fairies draw near,
And give the child good fortune.
Here, it is risky,
Risky in the world!
Broom and branches,
Dry more branches,
And yet more branches,
And yet more branches,
I give them to the fire!
O fire, O fire, burn!
Hear the tears of the child!

📖 Leland, *The English Gypsies,* 58–59; Marushiakova and Popov, "Legends," 30–31.

FISH (*matscho, motsche, tznefniakero*): If a person eats fish at midnight the dreams they have that night will come true sooner or later. The fish is also the symbol of stupidity for the Gypsies, and they have a proverb that says "Stupid as a fish, cunning as a fox."

A folktale tells us that a fish thrown back into the water by a young man gave him a scale with instructions to burn it near the river if he ever found himself endangered by water. In another tale a fish brings back a ring from the bottom of a lake.

✦ *Fish-Man*

📖 Wlislocki, *Volksdichtungen*, nos. 33, 91; Wlislocki, *Märchen und Sagen*, nos. 20, 47.

FISH-MAN: In a Russian variant of the legend of the pharaoh the troops of the Egyptian sovereign who were swallowed up by the Red Sea were transformed into beings that were half man and half fish (*paš manuša, paš mače*). Since that time they have been living amid the waves, where now and then they would question a fisherman: "When will we turn back into men again?" If the fisherman answered them that he did not know, in a fury they would unleash a tempest; but if they were given the answer "Tomorrow," they would sink beneath the waves, shouting, "Tsyganka (Gypsy in Russian), drop dead in prison!" Tsyganka is the name of the wife of Pharavono.

✦ *Pharavono*

📖 Berger, "Mythologie der Zigeuner," 791.

FLAME, LIGHT (*plameňa, báro chačerdi*): The presence of a flame indicates an enchanted place or a hidden treasure. When a lad digs at the spot where it has appeared he finds an iron door, enters, and discovers a dwarf that had been captured by the king of the weasels, whose wife he had slain. The boy learns that the light he had seen was the glow of a luminous ring, which the dwarf offers to him. By chance, the boy discovers that his hand fills with gold pieces whenever he turns the ring.

📖 Ficowski, *Le Rameau de l'arbre*, 210–14.

FLEA (pl. *pušuma;* sg. *pušum/pischommtzua*): Grubby (Kelálo) and Lazy were brother and sister, or cousins. They got married, but

God punished them, and Lazy gave birth to the fleas that spread and multiplied. An etiological legend recounts the following:

Grubby and his sister Lazy were driven out of a large town one day and wandered for a long time through the world, persecuted and mocked by men and beasts. After a long pilgrimage they made their way into a land where the sun always shone and where people lived happy, content lives without tiring themselves out working. Grubby then said, "It is nice and warm here, let's stay!" Lazy yawned and murmured, "It's all the same to me." Both of them settled down comfortably and lived for a long time in a good relationship. Grubby grew larger every day and was soon as big and fat as the fattest of butchers. On the other hand, Lazy did not change one single bit, and this vexed her greatly. She complained about it to her aunt Boredom, who said to her, "Listen, I have a great idea! You and Grubby should get married and then you will no longer have any cause to feel envious." And that is just what they did. Grubby and Lazy made a fine pair who lived happily and contentedly. But their bliss was short-lived, because Our Lord punished this marriage between a brother and a sister. When Lazy gave birth she brought into the world fleas, which grew and multiplied everywhere their parents went to live, much to the aggravation of their mother.

📖 Herrmann, *Märchen und Lieder der Roma*, 221–22; Wlislocki, *Märchen und Sagen*, no. 5.

FLOWER OF HAPPINESS: This is a blue flower with the ability to speak, which grows over the grave of a mother. It is invisible to everyone but her son, whom she leads to happiness, thereby playing the role of a benevolent fate. Implicit in this narrative is the reincarnation of a dead woman into a flower.

📖 Wlislocki, *Märchen und Sagen*, no. 13.

FLUTE (*lauta*): The Gypsies believe that this musical instrument was invented by Saint Peter. When he stumbled across a drunkard by the side of the road whom he mistook for a dead man, he brandished his staff in the air above him. As this staff was hollow, when Saint Peter heard the sounds it produced, he was inspired to create a flute.

📖 Wlislocki, *Volksdichtungen*, 65.

FOUR-EYED DOG: A female dog that had four eyes was living in the Blessed Mountains. When she slaked her thirst in the rivers it would start to rain. When she slept, only two of her eyes would close. The dog leaves her turds in front of the homes of men beloved by a fairy (Urme). If you find one when stepping out of your house you should touch it with your left foot; doing so will cause this foot to lead you toward great treasures.

The four-eyed dog sometimes mixes one of her puppies into the litter of another bitch. It is white as snow with black circles around its eyes.

One tale features this dog as the protector of a young woman who, thanks to her, is delivered from the hands of her abductor. The dog tears this man to pieces and then vanishes.

This animal corresponds to Indra's dog Sarama, ancestor of all canines. According to one hymn in the *Rig Veda* (VIII, 6, 15, 16) she gave birth to two puppies with four eyes, the Sarameya, who became the watchdogs of Yama, the god of the dead. In another part of the *Rig Veda* (X, 14, 10), in a song addressed to a dead person, we read: "May you escape from the two multi-colored dogs, sons of Sarama, the dogs with four eyes, on a blessed path."

✦ *Blessed Mountains, Urme*

📖 Wlislocki, *Aus dem inneren Leben,* 61; Wlislocki, *Volksdichtungen,* no. 56; Berger, "Mythologie der Zigeuner," 795–96; Willman-Grabowska, "Le Chien dans l'*Avesta* et dans les *Védas*," 30–67.

FROG (*capni, žamba,* **cf. Sanskrit** *jambūka*)**:** This is the form assumed by Ana, but it is also taken by the wicked *kešalyia* who are seeking to kill the dwarfs.

The frog is sometimes a young woman who has been transformed into an amphibian. The curse that has been cast upon her is broken when her skin is burned. As it becomes burnt, this skin turns into gold.

✦ *Ana, Engagement, Kešalyia*

📖 Wlislocki, *Volksdichtungen,* no. 64.

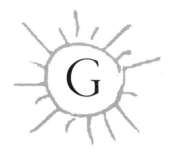

GARLIC (*siv, seria, sir, tzira, česnako*): Garlic has a variety of names among the Gypsies, such as *arimanakri,* coined from *armin Anakri,* "the herb of Ana" (Ana being the queen of the fairies). It is used to heal the bites caused by rabid dogs. Whenever a fire broke out in the village people would toss a clove of garlic over their roof to protect their homes.

Because Shilalyi was lashing out at the members of her family (all of whom were married while she remained a spinster), directing her spite especially at the children of her brother, who was mocking her, her brother gave their father a clove of garlic and advised him to urinate on it and then give it to his wife to eat. This was how Bitoso was born, who later became the husband of Shilalyi.

✦ *Ana, Bitoso, Melálo, Shilalyi*

📖 Wlislocki, *Aus dem inneren Leben,* 21–23, 178; Wlislocki, *Volksglaube,* 162.

GIRL WITH THE GOLDEN HAIR: ✦ Magical Conception, Star

GJEDDO ("God"): This name for the deity was collected by the missionary Thomas von Westen (1682–1727) from the Gypsies of the Trondheim region in Norway. It derives from the name of an ancient pagan god of the Lapps who was known as Kjedde or even Radien Kjedde.

📖 Etsel, *Vagabondenthum und Wanderleben in Norwegen,* 118.

GLOSSOPETRAE (*bicibakro bar*): Also known as "(serpent) tongue stones," if one of these stones is found on a blessed mountain it will dispel misfortune and illness. It also can be used as an oracle stone (as it shares the thoughts of King Sun, "who sees everything in the world") and is kept by the tribe as a relic. The Gypsies often confuse glossopetrae for the stones known as "thunderbolts" or "thunder stones" (*ceraunia*).

✦ *Blessed Mountain, King Sun, Thunder Stone*

📖 Wlislocki, "The Worship of the Mountains," 215; Wlislocki, *Aus dem inneren Leben,* 63–75; Berger, "Mythologie der Zigeuner," 811–12.

GLOWWORM (*grinda somnákube*): The Gypsies believe that this creature lingers around places where gold has been buried. When it dies, it transforms into gold.

📖 Wlislocki, *Vom wandernden Zigeunervolke,* 129.

GOD (*Devel, Del*): Before they used this term for the Christian deity, Gypsies used to designate as God everything that is above the Earth, whether the sun, the clouds, or the sky. There is the "great" or the "old god" (*baro, pharo devel*), in other words, God the Father; and the "little" or "young god" (*tikno, tarno devel*), meaning God the Son. The Transylvanian and Hungarian Gypsies believe that Christ began ruling because his father was either dead or he had abdicated.

The Gypsies think that the great God (*baro devel*) sends thunder and lightning, called the "fire of God" (*develeskero yak*), "God's weather" (*develeskero tsiro*), or "divine anger" (*develeskero tschingerpenn*). This god is the source of snow and rain (*miro baro devel dela gîb, dela berschindo*), and his lights (*develeskere momelinja*) are the stars that shine in the firmament.

📖 Schwicker, *Die Zigeuner in Ungarn und Siebenbürgen*, 153; Liebich, *Die Zigeuner in ihrem Wesen und in ihrer Sprache*, 31–32.

GOLDEN AGE: For many centuries human beings were happy and never wore any clothes, for there was neither cold nor snow; even the rain was lukewarm. But people insulted the great God (*baro devel*), and then distress, poverty, snow, cold, and wind appeared, which killed people like flies. Even the devils were freezing, which prompted them to go among men to obtain fire. Initially the humans refused them, but the devils offered to initiate men into two arts, that of the forge and that of sewing, and they got the fire they wanted.

✦ *Great Flood, Pharavono*

📖 Berger, "Mythologie der Zigeuner," 782.

GORGIO: This is the name that God gave to the first man. It should be noted that this name designates those who are not Gypsies, the *Gadjé* (sg. *Gadjo*).

✦ *Anthropogeny*

GOSPELS OF THE GYPSIES: According to Gypsy tradition the little God (*sunto del, tikno devel*) is the son of Sinpetra and Mary. On seeing that Mary was always attended by three doves wherever she went, God asked her if she was prepared to receive his breath (*duko*). She eventually acquiesced to his request and found herself pregnant. She gave birth in a stable with the help of Cretchuno's wife. At that moment a star, Netchaporo, appeared in the sky. "Its reflection, its emanation, is not merely a sign but an actual part of Him," says Zanko, the leader of the Kalderash. The godmother Mary cut off both her husband's hands because he had touched the newborn and thus defiled him.

However, when Cretchuno touched him again, his hands grew back.

When the Jews saw the star they grew alarmed and killed all their children, all of whose stars fell from the heavens while that of Sunto Del remained hanging in the sky.

The Jews caused even more suffering to Sunto Del, but he was never slain, and they eventually buried him alive. He overturned the stone placed over his tomb and climbed into heaven with Sinpetra, where he still reigns with him to this day.

✦ *Cretchuno, Netchaporo*

📖 *Zanko, chef tribal chez les Chalderash*, IV, 1–49; Michaelis, *Die apokryphen Schriften zum Neuen Testament*, 72–95.

GREAT FLOOD: One day during the Golden Age an old man came to the home of a couple and asked them if they could give him shelter for the night. He slept in their thatched cottage and was well treated by the wife. Before resuming his journey the next morning the old man gave his host a small fish in a bowl and ordered her to not eat it. But the woman ignored his command

and ate the fish, whereupon she was struck and killed by a bolt of lightning. This was the first death on Earth. Then it began raining without letup. When the old man returned some nine days later he advised the widower to remarry, gather up all his family, and build a boat because all of mankind was doomed to die by drowning. He told him to bring animals and seeds on board with them. After this it continued to rain for an entire year. When the waters again receded, everyone disembarked from the vessel into a new world where, from that point on, it was necessary to work, build, and sow crops in order to live.

This myth has a parallel version in the Indian legend about the great flood.

One day, while Manu was bathing in the river, he found a tiny fish. Manu brought the fish back home with him, where it grew and grew until one day it asked Manu to release him into the sea. Before swimming away, the fish warned Manu of an imminent deluge that would cover the entire Earth, and he advised the wise man to build a gigantic boat to protect himself. Manu heeded the fish's counsel and brought creatures and seeds aboard his ship. Shortly before his construction was completed, it began raining so hard that the Earth was soon flooded. The waters soon became rough, threatening to capsize the vessel. But Mataya appeared again, this time in the form of a gigantic fish, and towed the ship across the sea. He then advised Manu to moor the boat to the top of a mountain that had not been submerged and to wait there until the waters lowered. Before leaving, Mataya admitted to Manu that he was in fact Vishnu.

✦ *Golden Age, Pharavono*

📖 Wlislocki, *Märchen und Sagen,* no. 3; *Zanko, chef tribal chez les Chalderash,* 28–35; Berger, "Mythologie der Zigeuner," 812; Oişteanu, "The Romanian Legend of the Flood."

GROUYA: This is the name of a giant who, against the advice of his father, decides to civilize Novaca, "the great city" (*baro grado*), which Zanko says was located on the Bosphorus. Grouya gets so drunk, however, that the inhabitants of the city defeat him and throw him down a well. Using his own blood, Grouya writes a message that a raven carries to his father, who comes to the city to free him, and together they perpetrate a massacre there. The sovereign of Novaca finally realizes that he will be forced to do the "civilizing" of what remains of his people.

   📖 Berger, "Mythologie der Zigeuner," 808; *Zanko, chef tribal chez les Chalderash*, 120–23.

GUARDIAN SPIRIT: ✦ Butyakengo

GYPSY (*Rom;* fem. *Romni; Romnitschel, Romino*): It is commonly said that Gypsies are born on the grass of the steppes in the shadow of a solitary tree. The wind kisses their foreheads, the rain cleans and baptizes them, and the stork was their godmother. In Transylvania the Gypsies were born from a wise man and a disobedient wife whose husband condemned her to become datura. According to a Serbian etiology legend the Gypsies are the descendants of a one-eyed woman and a blind man. The first to be born was a daughter, and the second born was a son. At the behest of the Lord they married each other and had twins, who then left their parents. The twins were reunited some fifteen years later, married each other, and so on it continued until all forty-one Gypsy tribes had appeared.

According to other Serbian sources an old, paralyzed woman who was a surviving member of the Paravunore (Pharavono) was impregnated by the devil and gave birth to twins, the first ancestors of the Gypsies. The Gypsies of Turkey have another explanation for their origin, which was told in April 1887 by Hadji Hussein to Carnoy and Nicolaïdes.

Nemroud [Nimrod] the Infidel had made Abraham the Just his captive and wished to kill him by fire. He had a massive pyre built and set alight and commanded that Abraham be hurled onto it. The heat was so intense that no one could get close enough to toss Nemroud's prisoner into the fire.

"Build me a machine that can throw Abraham onto the pyre!" he ordered.

But no one was successful at constructing this machine. It was then that Satan presented himself to Nemroud the Infidel. "You will never be able to cast Abraham into your fire," the demon told him, "until a brother and a sister succumb to each other's lust!"

At once a man named Tchîn and his sister Guian prostituted themselves to each other. The child who was born from their incestuous union was called Tchinguiané, or Tchinguéné. He was the father of all the Gypsies.

In Russia it is said that Gypsies are descendants of the plum, which is why they have such deeply hued skin.

If the Gypsies are dark, wear tattered clothing, and wander all over the world, and if their name alone suffices to scare children, it is because they had already taken flight when God assigned a destiny to each people. Their faces were black and their clothing was torn. God therefore condemned them to keep this appearance.

The Slovenian variant recasts a widely spread European folktale and applies it to the Gypsies. In this version Gypsies are the children whom Adam and Eve hid from the eyes of God when he came to visit them. Irritated, God said that he would only take care of the children whom he saw, and those who had been concealed became Gypsies. They would live in the woods and have no houses. This legend can be found all over Europe and is not of Gypsy origin.

We learn this in a dialogue from the Slovak Gypsies:

Why do you call yourselves Siganes?
Because we like to create tales and *gausses* [jokes].
Why do you say that you are the sons of woman and not
of man?
Because the man is only a man after he has been conceived
by woman.

Another etiological legend maintains that the different tribes are the descendants of men whom a witch transformed into dogs. Once they regained their original human form they all went off in their separate directions to find their relatives, but all of the latter had long since died. These men are the ancestors of the people who form the various tribes today, who pursue different professions. They are the *ciobatori* (cobblers), *cotorari* (tinsmiths), *ghilabari* (musicians), *lautauri* (musicians and luthiers), *linguari* and *rudari* (craftsmen of wooden objects), *mečteri lacatuši* (locksmiths), *salahori* (masons), *ursari* (bear-tamers), *vatraši* (gardeners and farmers), and *zlatari* (gold-panners).

✦ *Datura, Pharavono, Rom*

📖 Wlislocki, *Volksdichtungen,* 187–89; Kabakova and Stroeva, *Contes et Légendes tsiganes,* 112–14; Kornel, "Gypsy Anecdotes from Hungary," 69–70; Nounev, "Legends," 49, 54; Haltrich, *Zur Volkkunde der siebenbürgischen Sachsen,* 119–20; Berger, "Mythologie der Zigeuner," 805; Groome, *Gypsy Folk-Tales,* 331–41; Carnoy and Nicolaïdes, *Folklore de Constantinople,* 14–15.

GYPSY DIASPORA: There are several different etiologies concerning the dispersal of the Gypsies throughout the world and their lack of any fixed abode. According to one legend, when the trades were being awarded to the different people a Gypsy hid behind God, who granted him a portion of what the people gathered there had received. This is why the Gypsies have no country, are scattered across the globe, and have to beg for their portion.

Another legend says how, when fleeing to escape the gaze of God, the Gypsies colored their faces black, tore their clothing, hid beneath a bridge, and waited. When God came along they tried to scare him. He looked at them and said, "Your fate will be to always roam!"

When God divvied up lands and goods he overlooked the Gypsies and gave them barren lands, authorizing them to steal and cheat. And when he gave everyone their share of destinies, the devil was their lot.

In the myth concerning the Egyptian origin of the Gypsies it is also said that Pharavono (Pharaoh) irritated Moses and that God then cursed him to wander over the Earth with his people.

✦ *Pharavono*

📖 Nounev, "Legends," 49; Kabakova and Stroeva, *Contes et Légendes tsiganes,* 67, 76; Kenrick and Golemanov, *Three Gypsy tales from the Balkans,* 60; Obert, *Rumänische Märchen und Sagen aus Siebenbürgen,* no. 30.

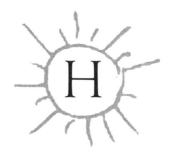

ḤÁGRIN: ✦ Chagrin

HAIR, FUR (*bal;* **cf. Sanskrit** *bāla, vāla*): A hair that has been cut into tiny pieces and mixed in with food will put dragons to sleep. The hairs from this monster that have been burned into ash and swallowed will provide humans with protection from their attacks. Moreover, if before swallowing them the individual thinks of a place where he or she would like to go, they will be immediately transported there. The hairs from the king of the devils' beard will change everything they touch into pure gold. Eating a hair from a fairy will make it possible to return from the Other World to the place whence you started.

When kept in a handkerchief, the beard and hairs of a dwarf will bring good luck.

To treat a child's stomachache, nine hairs from a black dog are reduced to ash while reciting a charm. These ashes are blended with mother's milk and some of the child's own excrement to form a paste that is then sealed within a hole in a tree.

A prince who had been born covered with hair and endowed with extraordinary strength, and who began talking and walking at birth, went to war against his father. In return for peace he demanded that a young woman eat his hairs. One day a poor girl accepted his demand. The lad cut off all his hair, had it ground together with flour, and she ate the cake that was baked from it. Immediately the boy transformed into a marvelously handsome young man.

Red hairs are regarded as a sign of good luck, and they are called *bálá kámeskro,* which means "the hairs of the sun."

✦ *Dragon, Leïla*

📖 Wlislocki, *Märchen und Sagen,* 24–29, 58–61; Wlislocki, *Volksdichtungen,* no. 38; Leland, *The English Gipsies and Their Language,* 25.

HALLA: The wife of King Serpent.

✦ *King Serpent*

HAZEL (*agor, kor*): Branches cut from a hazel tree during Lent will protect tents and buildings from lightning. The Gypsies who have settled in one place make brooms from hazel branches that they hang from the top of the roof.

📖 Wlislocki, *Volksglaube,* 146.

HAZELNUT: Because she ate a double hazelnut, a woman found herself pregnant and gave birth to a hazelnut and a little worm. She buried them in the forest, and a hazel tree grew out of the ground bearing a single hazelnut pierced with a hole. The hazelnut was the dwelling of her son and daughter, who could take on human shape once a day. After various events transpired, the two young people were able to rejoin the human community.

📖 Wlislocki, *Volksdichtungen,* no. 61.

HOLYIPI: ✦ Mountains of the Moon

HORSE (*grái, graj, grast*): Horses have the ability to see demons at night, and they also play an oracular role. If a horse rolls around in front of a tent or a house it is the herald of a death. If it neighs during the day the invalids can hope to be healed soon, bridegrooms will experience good fortune, and pregnant women will have an easy birth.

The horse plays a part in the rites of protection. On Pentecost sedentary Gypsies will plant horse skulls on stakes in front of their farm to protect them from demons and witches. The nomadic Transylvanian Gypsies, who spend their winters in caves, will bury the skull of a horse inside. The Gypsies of southern Hungary also place skulls like this on graves to prevent a devil or witch from trampling on it, for if these individuals could do this, the heart of the dead person would begin to burn and appear to its surviving relatives in the form of a tiny blue flame—a will-o'-the-wisp (*vodyi mulengré*, "the heart of the dead man"). To protect their animals from mange (*ger*), which is also called "witch's broom" (*motura bengeskro*), the Gypsies pour water through a horse skull several times. One never rides a horse when it has just crossed through a body of water by swimming because it will be carrying the saliva of the *nivaši*, and this can drive people mad. Horses are also used to perform a part of a circumambulation rite. Before setting up a camp the Gypsies will ride around the site astride a horse to prevent harm from befalling any horses or riders.

It should be noted that the cricket is called "God's little horse" (*devleskero grái*).

There is one Gypsy tale in which a horse's head invited a young fugitive to hide himself inside its left ear. The boy became tiny and entered the ear. Once the danger had passed he came out of the skull through the right ear and regained his normal size. The skull advised the boy to bring him along as he would provide him protection.

Another story tells how witches can transform men into horses by throwing a bridle around their necks.

✦ *Apple, Christmas, Mašurdalo, Mother of the Sun, Nivaši*

📖 Wlislocki, *Volksglaube,* 125–26; Wlislocki, *Vom wandernden Zigeuner-volke,* 129; Wlislocki, *Volksdichtungen,* nos. 34, 55, 63; Lecouteux, *The Tradition of Household Spirits,* 21, 38.

I

ILIA: This is the name of a judge from the Other World who travels across the Earth rewarding the good and punishing the wicked. The eldest of his wife's seven brothers visited him and revealed to him the existence of the purgatories and the paradises. 📖 *Zanko, chef tribal chez les Chalderash,* 103–10.

ILLITERACY: The Gypsies regard their lack of a written culture as a curse and have a number of legends that explain why this is so. One shows how Dundra, the messenger of God, revealed to them their secret laws and had them written down in a book. The Gypsies left India for Chaldea, but when this country could no longer feed them the mages ordered them to separate. The most courageous of them returned to India with the sacred books, and, today, no one knows what ever became of them.

According to another tradition, God came down to Earth to give the Gypsies an alphabet, but the only person he could find was an old man accompanied by a donkey, because everyone else had gone off to harvest the fruit of the blackthorn. He gave this old man the alphabet written out on a cabbage leaf, but the donkey ate it, and thus the Gypsies do no not have an alphabet.

Zanko, the leader of the Kalderash tribe, lamented in 1955: "We have no right to a script. This is our curse." According to another tradition it was their punishment for forging the nails that were used to crucify Christ. On the other hand, God awarded them the talent to know how to organize festivities and celebrations.

In 1837, Michel de Kogalnitchan (Mihail Kogălniceanu) observed: "The Gypsies still have no alphabet, and they undoubtedly will never have one, for as they become more civilized they will start experiencing new needs and will not feel the need to preserve a language as defective as theirs."

✦ *Alako, Pharavono*

📖 Berger, "Mythologie der Zigeuner," 810; Ville, *Tziganes,* 69–71; Kabakova and Stroeva, *Contes et Légendes tsiganes,* 68; *Zanko, chef tribal chez les Chalderash,* 13, 31; Kogalnitchan, *Esquisse sur l'histoire, les mœurs et la langue des Cigains connus en France sous le nom de Bohémiens,* 36.

IRON (*saster, trascht, trás*): When iron appears as the characteristic element of a building, the presence of this metal signals that the edifice belongs to the Other World. Wicked fairies, dragons, and the Čarana always live in an iron castle. When spitting on the earth three times after sowing datura seeds upon it, a dragon caused the emergence of men made of iron. Subterranean chambers and caves that house treasure are sealed by iron doors.

✦ *Čarana, Dragon, Urme*

JACK O' LANTERN, WILL-O'-THE-WISP: Jack o' Lantern is another name the English Gypsies have for the ghostly lights that are believed to be light-spirits or the spirits of the dwarfs.

✦ *Avali, Will o' the Wisp*

📖 Leland, *The English Gipsies and Their Language,* 241–43 (GUDLO XXXIV).

JIMSON WEED: To prevent the múlo from abducting their women on January 1, the Gypsies place jimson weed seeds, the herb of witches, beneath their beds.

✦ *Datura, Múlo*

JOSIPO: King of the Gypsies who lives in Kucela.

✦ *Curko*

JUKLANUŠ: ✦ Dog-Man

KAKAVA: This is a festival of the Turkish Gypsies of Edirne and Kirklareli that celebrates the end of their slavery in Egypt under the rule of Pharaoh. It takes place at the beginning of spring, several days after the Jewish holiday of Pesach (Passover).

✦ *Pharavono*

KEŠALYIA (sg. *kešalyi*): These are the daughters of King Mist, who drove them away from his palace after King Sun had burned his beloved wife. They live in mountains and forests, where they sometimes reside in palaces of gold and diamonds, and they let their hair hang down into the valleys. They can then be seen in the form of fog that the Gypsies call "hair of the *kešalyia*" (*Kešalyakri*). Their eyes shine with a green light. Sometimes it is they who weave the invisible caul (amniotic membrane) and guarantee a lifetime of good fortune for the individual so chosen. It is also said that they spin a "red thread of happiness" for the child to whom they wish to show their favor. This thread looks like a red line on the individual's throat. Or, they can slip a shirt woven from their own hair onto the selected individual—hair that is so fine that the shirt remains invisible—which will give good luck to its owner. Their nature as fates is attested to by their number: there are often three of them. When an individual dies suddenly it is said that he or she "has slept with the *kešalyi.*"

The *kešalyia* must visit the home of their queen, Ana, every day. There they each give her a drop of blood to drink from their left hand, otherwise she will die and the *loçolicos* will devour all the *kešalyia.* They sleep all winter in their caves until the first song of the cuckoo. This bird is a messenger: it spends the winter with them, and they send it off to see if spring has arrived.

A *kešalyi* can only love one single man. She will toss him a golden rope and hoist him to the top of the mountain. She will only bear one child from him. This child dies soon after its birth and is shortly followed into the grave by its father. Wild with grief, the *kešalyi* will flee higher into the mountain, and her cloak of mist will turn black. Some also say that the *kešalyia* disappear after they have given birth to a child. They also sometimes provide men with objects that help them successfully fulfill their quests, such as a balm that shatters chains.

Due to a magic spell revealed by a *phuvuš,* a *kešalyi* was forced to vanish. Her hair turned white, the glow of her eyes dimmed, and she sank into the ground along with her palace. When they have been abused or violated in any way the *kešalyia* will exact a terrible revenge.

Among the Gypsies of England, the *kešalgo* are the daughters of the mists. They will put a lost Gypsy back on the right path, provided he is savvy enough to address them in the "language of the spirits."

According to one etiological legend, a *kešalyi* played a key role in the formation of the tribe of Leïla. Exiled to the forest by her father, the princess Leïla was on the verge of dying of starvation when she received three hairs to eat from a *kešalyi.* She became pregnant, gave birth to a son, and then was killed by her father's henchmen. Her child escaped and established the tribe of Leïla.

Scholars have suggested two different etymologies for *kešalyi.* The name derives either from *keš,* meaning "silk," or from *keša,* meaning "hair." In the nineteenth century belief in the existence of the *kešalyia* was confirmed among the Gypsy tribes of the Danube and those of Transylvania and southern Russia. They can also be found in Poland and England.

✦ *Ana, King Mist, King Sun, Leïla, Loçolico, Pçuvuš*

📖 Wlislocki, *Aus dem inneren Leben*, 3, 133, 152–53; Wlislocki, *Volksglaube*, 11–21; Wlislocki, *Märchen und Sagen*, no. 12; Ficowski, *Le Rameau de l'arbre*, 68–72; Berger, "Mythologie der Zigeuner," 795–96.

KING FIRE (*Raj Yag*): He is the personification of the element of fire (*yag, yakh*) and is regarded as a sovereign. He is the youngest son of Earth. Because he is always cold, he makes his home in the depths of the Earth, from where he rarely emerges. The lightning bolts are his sons. When King Wind chases them they flee at top speed toward their father. However they sometimes become lost, fall to the earth at random, and become petrified. These "thunderbolts" or "thunder stones" (ceraunia) will emerge from the ground nine years later, and the person who finds one on a mountain will see all his undertakings crowned with success; he will be "blessed" (*baçtales*).

✦ *King Wind, Thunder Stone*

📖 Wlislocki, *Aus dem inneren Leben*, 50–51.

KING MIST (*Ráj Muçlyi, koeddo, vátola*): He is one of the sons of the Earth (Pçuv). He appears in the form of an old, gray-haired blind man who dwells in a cave guarded by wolves on the mountain. He owns a tree whose leaves drip water and produce the rainfall on Earth—or which he shakes to make it rain—and a herd of yellow cows whose horns hold rings. He also lives in the impassable crevasses and ravines of the mountains. In front of his home stands a tree that bears three golden apples guarded by dog-men. The first apple makes people wealthy, the second makes them happy, and the third brings them permanent good health. His daughters are the clouds that King Wind hunts and brings into the belly of the Earth, their grandmother. If his children encounter any danger between heaven and earth this grandmother tosses them a multicolored rope, the rainbow (*strafelyi*), and draws them to her. The servants of this king are Rain (Prischindo), Wind, Lightning (Dewleskeri jakh, meaning "Divine Fire"), Thunder (Tschetogasch, Gwittrolo), Hail (Schohsi, Grados), and Snow (Ieve, Iw).

He sometimes transforms into a gray horse. It is said that one of his daughters, or his wife, visited the land of men to learn love.

> "I live far from here, in the land of eternal snows," she told them. "There I heard tell that the inhabitants of this country know the love that makes them both happy and unhappy. I do not know what happiness is, I do not know what suffering is, and I know nothing of love. I would greatly like to feel the fires of passion, although I am numb and frozen, and my heart is paralyzed."

She married a young man of the tribe, and they had twenty children together. All blonds are their descendants.

✦ *Dog-Men, King Wind*

📖 Wlislocki, *Volksglaube,* 12, 25; Wlislocki, *Märchen und Sagen,* no. 2; Wlislocki, *Vom wandernden Zigeunervolke,* 265–66; Wlislocki, *Volksdichtungen,* 200.

KING MOON (*Ráj čon/Shon*): He is the moon that has been personified in the form of an adolescent man clad in silver. He owns a silver flute that lets people summon him when the person to whom he gave it in return for a good deed requires his aid. He also owns a coat that will carry people through the air.

He has two daughters who love to dance. One of them rewarded a musician who earned her favor by giving him a sickle that allows its wielder to slay a thousand men with one blow. The other one cursed a musician because he unintentionally caused the death of her sister. His punishment was to change his sex. But the deceased sister sent him a black horse with wings that allowed him to overcome a variety of ordeals.

Depending on the dialect, other names for "Moon" are *tschemul, mondo,* and *mrascha.*

📖 Wlislocki, *Volksdichtungen,* no. 34; Block, *Die materielle Kultur der rumänischen Zigeuner,* 181; Berger, "Mythologie der Zigeuner," 801; *Zanko, chef tribal chez les Chalderash,* 27, 93.

KING OF THE DWARFS: ✦ Čignomanuš, Mountain of Glass, Pani

KING OF THE EAGLES (*Ráj Bišolto, sháshos*): He lives in the Other World that is connected to the Earth by a dark hole in the heart of a tall mountain. His dwelling stands in the middle of a green meadow and gleams like gold. His land is that of immortality. The King of the Eagles possesses the Water of Life. A feather from his left wing will allow the people he has abducted to return to their world by flying. The people upon whom he lets his droppings fall become petrified.

📖 Wlislocki, *Volksdichtungen,* no. 49.

KING OF THE SHADOWS (*O Tinia*): This mysterious figure is a monster who gouged out the eyes and cut off the feet of two of his sisters and changed the third into a mare, in whose milk he bathed. In the tale he swallowed both the hero and his steed, but the hero set a fire inside his belly. He exploded with a huge noise and left behind the large pile of gold he had held inside.

📖 Wlislocki, *Volksdichtungen,* no. 45.

KING OF THE WATERS: ✦ Moon

KING OF THE WOLVES: He alone has the authority to make certain that wolf-men remain in their human form; he does this by stripping them of their wolf skins, which he personally burns. A female wolf who had been captured by a young miller, who had also taken away her skin, was forced to marry the miller, but one day she recovered her wolf hide and returned home to her fellow wolves. The miller asked the King of the Wolves to return his wife to him, but the king demanded that he first recognize her among the pack, and if he could not, he would be eaten. The miller identified his wife successfully and was allowed to leave with her.

📖 Wlislocki, *Volksdichtungen*, no. 65.

KING SERPENT (*Ráj Zap*): After he created man God created Šerkano, the King Serpent, and his wife, Halla, to test the strength of human beings. Šerkano and Halla correspond, respectively, to Satan and Lilith in the Hebrew tradition.

📖 Jangil, *Voyage maison*, 79; Zanko, *chef tribal chez les Chalderash*, 208.

KING SUN (*O Kham*): He is the personification of the sun and is regarded as a sovereign, the son of Earth and Sky. The Romani name comes from the Sanskrit *gharma*, "heat." In the morning he is a little child, at midday he is a very handsome young man clad in glittering garments, and in the evening he is a weak old man who ends his course across the heavens to go sleep in the bosom of his mother. If he is prevented from sleeping he will remain old and without strength, and he will not be able to rise the next day. His primary enemy is his brother King Wind. Like both of his brothers he owns a flute, although his is made of gold, and he owns a herd of white cattle that wear gold rings. When he decided to get married he charged his eagle with the task of abducting the most beautiful of all the fairies.

In his kingdom there grows a tree whose leaves are stars and whose flowers are small moons. It is guarded by four white dogs who shoot bolts of lightning from their eyes and whose barking is like thunder. One of its branches makes it possible to bring the dead back to life. A variant story tells how King Sun offered one of its branches to a one-eyed man who used it to procure immortality for the inhabitants of his country. King Sun transformed the lands of a king who had offended him into a burning desert and transformed its sovereign into a man with a bird's beak. He only regained his original form when his wife, whom he had abandoned because she had broken a taboo, succeeded in finding him again after having worn out nine pairs of iron shoes on her search.

Cham Sun

The mountains created by King Sun are sacred. He is the protector of wild animals. When a hunter kills an animal he buries its bones, claws, fur, and teeth in the Blessed Mountains in order to appease him.

It is believed that when a bird of prey flies over a wedding it is a sign that the daughters of King Sun disapprove of the union and refuse to give it any happiness. This couple must then travel to the Blessed Mountains without any delay and leave a chicken tied to a stake there.

✦ *Blessed Mountains, Flute, King Wind*

📖 Wlislocki, *Aus dem inneren Leben,* 126; Wlislocki, "The Worship of the Mountains," 215; Wlislocki, *Märchen und Sagen,* no. 8; Wlislocki, *Volksdichtungen,* no. 67; Groome, *Gypsy Folk-Tales,* 133–37, 283–88.

KING WIND (*Ráj Bavol, O Bavol*): He is the wind personified and is regarded as a sovereign, the strongest of the five sons of the Earth and Sky. All of the high mountains are his property. He creates the lightning bolts that his brother King Sun uses to give good fortune and oracles to human beings. He appears in the form of a handsome young man. He owns a flute made of iron that he will give to the individual who has proved helpful to him. It will summon him when needed.

📖 Wlislocki, *Märchen und Sagen*, 21–24.

KUKUYÁ: This is the name of a Gypsy tribe whose ancestors were born from the union of a *pçuvuša*—a dwarf woman—and a handsome young man she had found to her liking. She was already married, but her husband allowed her to live with the lad for ten years, provided that she promised to give him any children she had with him. They drew lots: her husband would get any daughters

she had with her young man, and she would keep all the sons. The *pçuvuša* awoke the young man, offered him much gold and silver, and he accepted her proposition. They lived together for ten years, and she gave him ten sons. Disconsolate at not having any daughters, the *pçuvuša* brought her husband underground while weeping "kuku-kukuyá," and her ten sons decided to call themselves Kukuyá.

✦ *Pçuvuša*

📖 Wlislocki, *Vom wandernden Zigeunervolke,* 69–70.

LADYBUG: The Gypsies call this beetle "God's little worm" (*kirmoro devlerkero*). According to one belief gold is buried at the spot where several ladybugs are found together.

 📖 Wlislocki, *Volksdichtungen,* 89.

LARK (*fecke*): Hearing the lark's song the first time you leave your house brings good luck; it provides wealth and wisdom. If someone kills a lark misfortune will befall their children, because, according to a legend, the first lark couple was a man and woman who quarreled incessantly with God because of their children, and he eventually transformed them. There is a proverb that says: "Give bread to the children and do not beat the lark!" (*De máro ráleske, te ná márá fecke!*).

 The lark is the favorite bird of the deceased souls who have not yet made their way into the Other World. On Pentecost people place lark eggs against a tree or stone at dawn; the number of eggs they set down corresponds to the number of dead in the family.

 📖 Wlislocki, *Volksdichtungen,* 305; Wlislocki, *Vom wandernden Zigeuner-volke,* 126, 160.

LEÏLA: This is the name of a tribe that was born from the hair of a fairy (*kešalyi*) that had been ingested by a young princess driven away from her home by her stepmother.* The young girl moved in to a cave at the edge of the forest on the border of the kingdom. The fairies of destiny (*kešalyia*) noticed her presence, and one of them told her sisters, "I am going to cast one of my hairs into the valley; she will eat it and give birth to a son who will take care of her." The second sister said, "I will make a golden stream flow past the entrance of her cave and plant a golden tree that will bear all the fruits of the earth." The third fairy, who was ill-intentioned, cast a curse: "I will see to it that luck never smiles upon this child when he grows up." The young woman gave birth to a son with a purple birthmark on his throat and realized who had given her this child. He grew up in one fell swoop when bathing in the golden river. But Leïla's brother learned that she was living there and sent his soldiers, who became intoxicated on the wine of the stream and slew Leïla. Her son escaped, got married, and decided that his people would call themselves Leïla in honor of his mother.

It should be noted that in Arabic ليلى, Leïla means "night."

✦ *Kešalyia*

📖 Wlislocki, *Vom wandernden Zigeunervolke*, 70–72.

LIFE (*tschiwepènn*), DURATION OF: According to the Serbian Gypsies, in the beginning man lived for one hundred years, but he asked God to let him live for an even longer time. Never satisfied, he eventually wearied God, who decided that humans would live no more than one lifetime each.

The Gypsies of Bulgaria have another tradition in this regard. At his birth the human being received twenty years of life and complained mightily about it. The donkey heard him and gave him twenty years of its life, but the human being continued to gripe. The ape then heard him and gave him twenty years of his life; then the human being was satisfied. Since that time he lives

---

*[In some tales it is her father, the king, who banishes her. —*Trans.*]

twenty years as a human, twenty years as an ass, and twenty years as an ape.

Originally, when a man died God would bring him back to life at a later time, but when he saw two sisters kiss their resurrected brother while holding a scarf over their mouths God became so irate at the sight of their disgust that he ceased reviving human beings.

📖 Kabakova and Stroeva, *Contes et Légendes tsiganes*, 129.

LIGHTNING, THUNDERBOLTS (*bleskos, vilamo*): Streaks of lightning, which are also called "God's Fire" (*develeskri jak*), are the sons of King Fire. They love to frolic with the clouds, but King Wind pursues them and drives them away toward their mother, the Earth, and they return to her bosom. If they get lost and fall at a bad spot while they are fleeing they will become instantaneously petrified and turn in to "thunder stones" (*ceresrobara*).

If they encounter any danger in their flight between the sky and earth, their grandmother (the Earth) throws them a multi-colored rope—the rainbow—and pulls them to her.

For protection against lightning the Gypsies of southern Hungary bury nettles, datura seeds, and pine boughs in their cabins (*kólyva*). Those from the north bury an egg from a black hen at the four corners of their home. Gypsies elsewhere do the same with an unbaked brick, carved with the symbol below.

In Transylvania the Gypsies who have settled in one location cast tablets into the fire, which have been steeped for nine days in holy water and bear the carved symbols below.

Branches from a hazel tree that have been cut during Holy Week possess the same power.

✦ *Ceresrobara*

📖 Wlislocki, *Aus dem inneren Leben,* 50–51, 152, 162–65.

LILI ("the Muddy One"): This is the daughter of Ana and Loçolico. She is the sister to Melálo, another demon of disease, as well as being his wife. She causes coughs, diarrhea, and catarrh—ailments that are termed the "phlegmy illnesses" (*lilye nahvalipena*)—in both men and animals. She is depicted as a fish with a human head with long hair. There is a legend that explains why she looks this way. When Melálo was seeking a wife and could not find one, Ana, his mother, advised him to catch a fish, cook it in the milk of a female donkey, and then pour a little of that milk in her vagina when she was sleeping. Nine days later Ana gave birth to a fish-girl.

Lili

The union with her brother resulted in the birth of minor demons that remain nameless and who possess their parents' abilities, although to a lesser extent.

✦ *Ana, Loçolico, Melálo*

📖 Wlislocki, *Aus dem inneren Leben,* 8–10.

LOÇOLICO, LOḤOLIČO, LUCA: This is the name for human beings who have been transformed by the devil into horrible creatures. Their bodies are covered with coarse, thick hair; they have long ears; their arms are twice as long as a human's; and their legs are like beanpoles. Their strength resides in the soles of their feet. If someone burns any of their hair the *loçolico* will die. The demons incinerate it, spread its ashes over other men who have signed a contract with the devil, and turn them into *loçolicos.* Their king has a pair of wings that allow him to move with the speed of the wind.

One day the king of the *loçolicos* fell in love with Ana, the queen of the *kašalyia,* who pushed him away before locking herself inside her black and impregnable castle. In revenge he and some of his fellows devoured several *kašalyia* and then threatened to eat all of the rest, but Ana consented to marry the king. It is from their union that the demons of illness were born. As the *loçolicos* have no partners, they urinate on the young women whom they have abducted, change them into mares, and then kill them by having intercourse! They are also called "the people of the serpent."

The *loçolicos* possess extraordinary strength and are able to uproot the largest of oak trees. By clapping his hands, one of them made a chariot appear, which is drawn by three scrawny nags, to transport the tree. They are ready to richly reward anyone who brings them the claw of a *chagrin.*

✦ *Kešalyia, Chagrin*

📖 Wlislocki, *Aus dem inneren Leben,* 3–4; Wlislocki, *Volksdichtungen,* nos. 25, 26, 32.

LOLMIŠO: This is Ana's seventh child. As the name indicates, she bears the shape of a mouse. Lolmišo was born because her mother was upset with her children and developed a skin rash. Her son Melálo advised her to have it licked by mice, and this was how Lolmišo came to be born. She carries diseases of the skin and infects the people she passes over at night while they are sleeping. Her victims can be cured by washing their skin with lukewarm water in which lentils and bat guts have been boiled, and after this liquid is poured into the hole of a tree while saying, "May Lolmišo come and devour this tree as long as you remain inside it!" This should be repeated every morning before sunrise, because that is when the demons of diseases are resting, exhausted and weakened from their nocturnal activities.

This name is formed from *lolo,* meaning "red," and *mishos,* "mouse."

✦ *Melálo*

📖 Wlislocki, *Aus dem inneren Leben,* 23.

MAGICAL CONCEPTION: A queen who had long been without children went to consult an old woman who was supposed to know some magic that might help her. This woman told her: "If you wish to have a daughter I can help you, but you will never have a boy. On the night of Holy Friday, shortly before midnight, go to the cemetery by yourself and dig up the bone of a hanged man there and bring it back home. On the day of Easter reduce it to ashes. Then take the hair of a young girl who is seven years, seven months, seven weeks, and seven days old and combine the hair with the ashes, boil them together in a stewpot with datura seeds, eat this gruel, and you will give birth to a girl." The queen faithfully followed this prescription and gave birth to a rose that transformed into a woman when a young man kissed and played a tune for her on his violin.

In another text a woman presented her husband with the egg of a black hen to eat right at the time of the full moon, and nine months later she gave birth to a young girl who possessed extraordinary gifts. When she fixed her hair, gold dust would fall from it; when she laughed, pearls would come out of her mouth; when she wept, tears of wine spilled from her eyes; and whenever she wished it, she could make flowers spring up beneath her feet.

✦ *Datura*

📖 Wlislocki, *Märchen und Sagen,* no. 21; Wlislocki, *Volksdichtungen,* no. 53.

MAGICAL OBJECT AND ELEMENT: Thanks to items of a magical nature the heroes of the tales can successfully achieve their quests, extricate themselves from sticky predicaments, and acquire happiness and wealth. For example, an egg from an ant permits a hero to call the ant people to his aid; a feather from the left wing of the King of the Eagles allows him to fly through the air; by using a magic mirror, two brothers discover what had happened to their youngest brother; another mirror will petrify anyone who gazes into it; a balm restores life to the dead and another will cause all chains to burst; a shawl makes its wearer invisible; a cloud carries the wife of King Mist; a silver flute permits a hero to call King Moon to his aid and to flee by flying away on a cloak; a potion or a needle will plunge a person into magical slumber; blowing on the hair from the beard of a dwarf (Čignomanuš) will cause him to appear; a certain kind of water will transform stones into pure gold; a magic rifle never misses its target; the water from a certain spring makes whoever bathes in it beautiful, while another spring grants wisdom, and a third restores sight; a magic rope used to encircle a garden prevents any intrusion; by ingesting the heart of a certain bird, a person can know what is being plotted against him or her; a marvelous sack refills itself with all the foods one wishes to eat; a ring turned from right to left will cause a ducat to appear in one's hand; a cauldron resurrects the dead; and the nails, hair, and beard of a dwarf are good luck charms.

✦ *Čignomanuš, Egg, King Moon, Ogre*

📖 Wlislocki, *Volksdichtungen,* nos. 44, 49, 52; Wlislocki, *Märchen und Sagen,* nos. 2, 11, 12, 13, 17, 22, 23, 26, 76, 77.

MAGPIE (masc. *kačkaráko; acla*): This bird is a good omen if it flies in from the right side; if it arrives from the left side it signals misfortune and death. In summer its call is a herald of rain; in the winter its cry means a spell of mild weather is due. Generally its presence is seen as forewarning of a death.

📖 Wlislocki, *Vom wandernden Zigeunervolke,* 123.

MAN IN THE MOON: Once upon a time men enjoyed a pleasant life in the moon as their only task there was to keep the fire going that produced its light. But an evil man who hated his fellow men banished them from the moon. To have light and heat he was then forced to maintain the fire and was constantly hunting for wood. The poor exiles of the moon dispersed across the sky—they are the stars and planets—and can be seen carrying bundles of sticks.

📖 Leland, *The English Gipsies and Their Language,* 323.

MAN OF THE WOODS (*vosesko manuš*): This is a giant with shaggy hair who lives in the caves of the mountain. He does not speak and only utters some inarticulate sounds. He sleeps on a sheepskin and comes down into the villages at night. Despite his great strength, a dog can drive him away. He is most likely identical to the *mašurdalo.*

✦ *Mašurdalo*

📖 Berger, "Mythologie der Zigeuner," 808.

MARRIAGE OF THE TREES (*biya kashtengre*): On Christmas Eve the nomadic Gypsies of Transylvania plant a small willow on the hill closest to their dwellings and tie knots on its branches. Next to it they plant a small fir tree, and the two trees are tied together with a red string. They call this the "Marriage of the Trees" and say that this rite traces back to an extremely ancient legend, that of the Tree of All Seeds. This legendary tree will often appear in the proximity of the married trees; anyone who sees it will be lucky or fortunate for the rest of their life—but they must not utter a single word until the tree disappears, otherwise they will go mad.

The next day the married trees are burned while the adults dance in a line, singing:

> *Múlo, múlo, múlo,*
> *Kana kate tu sal,*
> *Kana tute bokhala,*
> *Kay tu ças çabena,*
> *Ava katen hey' ava:*
> *Kate mas te marikla!*
> *Na barvalyol tu nascipa!*
> *Andro nevo Krishtekro!*

> Múlo, múlo, múlo
> If you are near,
> If you are hungry,
> Eat all the dishes,
> Come out, show yourself:
> Here is meat and bread!
> Do not increase our destitution!
> In the name of Christ!

They then bury the meat for the *múlo*. The ash of the trees is collected, and the chief of the tribe puts a little of it into his boots.

Serbian and Hungarian Gypsies surround several trees with a string, and while the tribe is kneeling the chief recites a prayer that is repeated by all present.

> *Baro ray andro ceros, amen! sam core kirmora andre pçuv!*
> *Amenge hin shil te bokh te trush te amen jiden sar core cirikleya; uva amen kamen te asharen tut!*

Miseça palalen amenge e ñiko sastyarel corenge!
Barvala pçurden te menge hin shil te ñiko sastyarel amenge:
oh baro ray bica kiya men t'ro gule caes, the amenge sascipen
hin, the miseça amenge naylashen! Amen.
Vay cores hin, sar yevende kirmora te tut amen taysa asharen,
oh baroray andro ceros!

We are cold, hungry and thirsty, and live like the poor birds, but we love you and praise you!

The evil spirits persecute us and no one helps us, poor us!

The winds blow and we freeze, and no one helps us!

O great lord, send us your dear son so that we may remain in good health and so that the evil [spirits] cause us no harm! Amen.

We are as poor as the worms in winter and yet, we continue to praise you, great lord of the sky!

✦ *Múlo, Tree of All Seeds*
📖 Wlislocki, *Volksglaube*, 137–41.

MAŠURDALO/MAŠMURDALO: This is a simpleminded and gullible giant with a weakness for human flesh, provided it comes from a healthy man. His name is a compound of *maš*, "meat," and *murdalo*, "killer." He haunts the woodlands and deserts, on the lookout for animals (he abducts sheep) and humans. He has a wife and children. His life is located inside an egg guarded by a hen; to slay Mašurdalo this egg must be destroyed. Because he has scant intelligence humans find it child's play to deceive him. He will show his gratitude to anyone who lends assistance in a perilous situation. He owns a bridle that will transform him into an ugly, scrawny horse if it is placed around his neck—but one that is as fast as the wind. Whoever drinks his blood will acquire enormous strength. It is said that he possesses huge treasures. He seeks to capture women to marry them. In one tale he gives good advice to a young man who wishes to gain the three golden apples on the Tree of All Seeds that stands inside the Golden Mountain guarded by nine black dogs and a dragon. Mašurdalo's family also owns the egg of the thousand-year-old owl, in which the worm of happiness can be found.

In a tale collected by Wlislocki we find a family of Mašurdalo who do not correspond to the preceding description. The mother has hair that shines like the sun and when questioned about this she replies, "I bring day to the world and take away the night."

Among the Serbian Gypsies, Mašurdalo takes the form of a robust man of the woods (*vošeko manuš*) who dwells inside a cave, sleeps on a sheepskin, and can only speak in grunting noises. A dog will put him to flight when he goes down to the villages at night to look at the dwellings of men.

Oddly enough, a charm against fever ends with an appeal to him for aid (*Mashurdalo sastyár!*). Another charm for healing a hernia goes like this:

Mašurdalo, tu sal sorales, me dav tu m're nashlyipen! Kana tu ada na kames, de tu ada tire romñi ada na kamel, yoy del ada leske caveske! Kana cavo ada na kamel, yoy del ada rukeske!

Mašurdalo, you are strong, I give you my pain! If you have no use for it, give it to your wife! If she has no use for it, may she give it to her son! If her son has no use for it, may he give it to this tree!

✦ *Man of the Woods, Tree of All Seeds, Worm of Happiness*

📖 Berger, "Mythologie der Zigeuner," 807; Wlislocki, *Volksglaube*, 26–27; Wlislocki, *Volksdichtungen*, nos. 19, 20, 50; Wlislocki, *Volksglaube*, 164; Leland, *Gypsy Sorcery and Fortune Telling*, 16–17.

MATUYÁ: This is the name of the queen of fairies and the sworn enemy of mice. She corresponds to Mautia of the Albanian Gypsies. The Gypsies of Turkey tell how an emperor wished to marry her, but she demanded a crown of mice so huge that it would encircle his entire kingdom. He was just on the verge of succeeding when the devil called all the mice of the world to the rescue by playing his violin (*shetra*). They invaded the kingdom, whereupon the devil made them devour the emperor.

To treat weeping abcesses the Serbian Gypsies cover them with a piece of red cloth that has been cut into the shape of a mouse. It is then buried in the ground (this is the magical therapeutic process that scholars designate as *transplantatio morbi*) while a charm is spoken that asks the nine Urme to bind Lolmišo by recalling the preceding legend.

According to another legend it was Matuya who would have played a role in the creation of the violin by giving a wooden box and a lock of her hair to a young man. After she both laughed and cried inside the box, the violin had the virtue of making people feel joyful or sorrowful.

Matuyá appears in the following, saying, "Matuya did it and the man laughed" (*Matuyá kerelás te mánush áshelás*), which refers to a person who has obtained something without making any effort.

✦ *Lolmišo, Urme, Violin*

📖 Wlislocki, *Aus dem inneren Leben*, 24; Wlislocki, *Vom wandernden Zigeunervolke*, 154, 222; Wlislocki, *Volksdichtungen*, no. 11.

MELÁLO ("the Dirty One"): This was the first child of the king of the *loçolicos* (intermediary demons) and Ana, the queen of the *kešalyia* (fairies of the mountains). He is depicted as a small, gray, two-headed bird that takes possession of people and causes madness, inciting them to murder and theft.

His claws are as sharp as razor blades; when he flies he spreads

Melálo

a sleep-inducing mist that causes people to go mad when they wake up.

◆ *Garlic, Kelšalyia, Loçolico*

📖 Wlislocki, *Aus dem inneren Leben,* 126; Wlislocki, "The Worship of the Mountains," 215; Wlislocki, *Märchen und Sagen,* no. 8; Wlislocki, *Volksdichtungen,* no. 67; Groome, *Gypsy Folk-Tales,* 133–37, 283–88.

MOON (*on/shone/tshonn* [cf. Sanskrit *chandra*]; *dude, mrascha*): This celestial body is personified in the form of a king, one of the five sons of Earth and Sky, and the father of the stars. This king had two daughters. One of them offered a silver flute to a Gypsy with whom she had fallen in love; he left her, and she died of grief. Her sister transformed the young man into a woman, and he only recovered his male appearance after he had eaten the golden apples of King Mist.

Schion or shonuto (schon):
Moon

The phases of the moon are caused by the Čarana. With the help of the King of the Waters (Pani; cf. Sanskrit *pānīya,* "waters") it rules the waters. According to another legend Saint Nicholas condemned a man who had no generosity to live on the moon and eat it, but God caused it to be unceasingly reborn.

The Gypsies believe that one should not walk bareheaded in the moonlight, otherwise one will go bald or grow old prematurely.

According to one legend a large number of human beings lived happily on the moon in ancient times, but there was a trouble-maker among them who chased everyone else away. Since that time he has been condemned to perpetually gather wood to make a fire so that he will not remain in darkness and die from the cold. And the poor folk he expelled from the moon are still traveling through the heavens: they are the stars and the other celestial bodies that are visible to us.

✦ *Čarana, King Mist*

📖 Wlislocki, *Volksdichtungen,* 106; Wlislocki, *Märchen und Sagen,* nos. 2, 8; Wlislocki, *Volksglaube,* nos. 12, 25; Berger, "Mythologie der Zigeuner," 801.

MOTHER OF TIME (*daj asos/čiro*): This figure appears in the shape of a serpent who is continually occupied with eating its own tail, which always grows back immediately. This clearly resembles the Ouroboros (οὐροβόρος), a symbol that we know existed in Egypt as far back as the fifteenth century BCE. According to a tale collected from the Hungarian Gypsies this serpent is covered with lice, and it will answer the questions of anyone who gets rid of them.

📖 Wlislocki, *Volksdichtungen,* no. 44.

METEORITE: King Sun has three daughters who are the most beautiful women in the world. They fly through the air during the day and enjoy tossing black, burning stones at people. As for the Moon, she gave birth to so many stars that soon her house was over-flowing with them. When she flies into a rage she will occasionally cast one down to Earth, and these are what we know as comets.

✦ *Comet, King Sun*
📖 Wlislocki, *Aus dem inneren Leben,* 67.

MINČESKRE (*Vulva*): This is a demoness, the eighth daughter of Ana, the queen of the *kešalyia.* She carries syphilis and skin diseases when she travels over people's bodies at night in the form of a beetle. She married Lolmišo, and with him she bore many children who cause skin disorders such as wens and pustules.

✦ *Kelšalyia, Lolmišo*
📖 Wlislocki, *Aus dem inneren Leben,* 25–26.

MOUNTAIN (*bergos, monta, hedo, themlin, rés*): The mountains were born when Earth and Sky separated. The Sky carried off their three children, King Sun, King Moon, and King Mist, but they held on tightly to their mother's garment, and the parts they pulled up formed the mountains. The Earth left them as they were so she could remain close to her children, but she peopled their summits with fairies (*kešalyia*) and spirits who would prevent her children from ripping her garment to pieces.

There is a tradition among the Bulgarian Gypsies that the Earth was originally flat. When God rose up the Earth followed him because it was his creation. God noticed this and stopped. The portions of the Earth that had already been lifted became frozen in that position, and this is why we have mountains and valleys today.

Only the mountains raised by King Sun are sacred, and seven of them are especially holy. They are called the Blessed Mountains (*baçtalo bar*), because everything that is undertaken in their radius is synonymous with success and good luck. But no one knows exactly where they are. At their feet flow springs whose waters possess healing properties. People must take pains to avoid defiling these mountains or entering them while chewing or forgetting to spit (*tchungaráva*), otherwise the careless individual can attract an incurable disease. The Gypsies associate the mountains of King Wind with their parents and grand-parents who thus have a Father Mountain and Mother Mountain with whom they commune.

The middle-size mountains are called the "Mountains of Evil," which is to say "of the demons" because these are the regions where such creatures reside. In ancient times the demons were still able to settle on the Blessed Mountains, but one day the Earth Mother became angry with her son King Moon, for-bidding him to see her when it was day, and she banished the demons to the Mountains of the Moon. When a Gypsy passes by a Mountain of the Moon he spits three times to avoid being captured by a *múlo*.

◆ *Blessed Mountains, Kešalyia, King Moon, King Sun, Múlo*

📖 Berger, "Mythologie der Zigeuner," 789; Wlislocki, "The Worship of Mountains," 211–19; Wlislocki, *Aus dem inneren Leben,* 66; Groome, *Gypsy Folk-Tales,* 108; Marushiakova and Popov, "Legends," 30–31.

MOUNTAIN OF GLASS: This is the mountain where a dragon guards three young women who are the most beautiful in the world. At nightfall they go to a lake in the form of golden geese. To free them the hero in this tale appeals to the dwarfs for aid, and they undermine the mountain for him. The mountain col-lapses, and the geese fly away. The dragon then attacks the hero, who slays the worm with a rifle that never misses its target, a weapon that was given to him by the king of the dwarfs.

◆ *Čignomanuš*

📖 Wlislocki, *Märchen und Sagen,* no. 13.

MOUNTAINS OF KING WIND: These are the highest mountains of all, and they are the place where the Gypsies believe the kingdom of the dead is located.

📖 Wlislocki, *Aus dem inneren Leben,* 72; Wlislocki, *Vom wandernden Zigeunervolke,* 298–304; Wlislocki, *Volksglaube,* 96–102.

MOUNTAIN OF THE CATS (*Bar makengre*): This mountain stands in the Other World, behind a great forest, and hundreds of cats dwell there. They are all souls of the dead who committed numerous sins when they were alive. They are obliged to remain there for many years until they are able to reach the kingdom of the dead (*them mulengre*). This mountain is girded by a wall of fire that only goes out on St. John's Night. A glittering stone can be found there that will open anything that is closed and transform any metals that it touches into gold. To any woman who agrees to enter their service, the dean of cats gives a stone that will transform into gold any piece of iron it touches under the new moon. Furthermore, this stone makes it possible to open up the ground and free any person that has been abducted and imprisoned there by a *pçuvuš*.

✦ *Pçuvuš*

📖 Wlislocki, *Volksdichtungen*, no. 42; Wlislocki, *Aus dem inneren Leben*, 71–72.

MOUNTAINS OF THE MOON (*Bar coneskro, Coneya*): This is the term the Gypsies use to designate the smallest mountains. They were born when King Moon ripped the garment of the Earth, his mother. These mountains are also the abode of devils, which is why they are also called the Mountains of Demons (*Bara miseçengre*). This is where the demons immigrated once they were expelled from the Blessed Mountains by Earth and King Moon. Witches (*holyipi*) hold their sabbaths here on a Friday night when they renew their pact with the devil by having him drink the menstrual blood they have set aside for seven years. Sacrifices to the moon are also made on these mountains.

A luminous plant that can impregnate women without sexual congress grows on these mountains. This is why people say of an unmarried woman who becomes pregnant: "She has inhaled the flower of the moon" (*yoy luludyi coneskro sungadyas*). A stone, muscovite, is also found on the Mountains of the Moon, which can be discovered on nights when the moon is shining. It glitters then, and its possession gives its holder a magical power of attraction. Only women have the right to collect it, so they always have large numbers of suitors!

It is not recommended to make fires on these mountains, because the demons (*miseç*) and the witches (*holyipi*) will gather the remnants and then sprinkle them over people while they are sleeping, thereby causing abscesses to appear. When departing these mountains it is imperative that one does not look back, otherwise witches will appear who spit a fatal poison.

✦ *King Moon*

📖 Wlislocki, *Aus dem inneren Leben*, 66–70.

MOUSE (*germuso, germesso, carmus, suretta*): Whoever rips out and ingests one of the three hairs that grow beneath the tongue of the red mouse will then be able to understand the language of the birds. This hair cannot be pulled out without the animal's consent, which is thereby showing its gratitude toward the individual for giving it food.

📖 Ficowski, *Le Rameau de l'arbre*, 87.

MÚLO ("spirit, ghost"): Originally, *múlo* simply meant a dead person. According to Zanko, the tribal leader of the Kalderash, it was the wandering soul of an evil man who came to haunt the living. A distinction is made between the white *múlo* (*parno múlo*) and the black *múlo* (*kalo múlo;* cf. Sanskrit *kāla,* "black"), with the latter, of course, being evil.

The black *múlo* has become a sort of vampire who has emerged from a stillborn child. It will grow for about thirty years before going on into the kingdom of the dead. It has no bones, and its hands possess no middle fingers, as it was forced to leave them behind in the grave. It lives in the mountains and keeps guard over the treasures it has stolen over the course of its nocturnal wanderings. Every year, on its birthday, one of its fellow *múlo* will cook it so as to restore its strength. It will sometimes abduct a woman, but this is only possible on January 1. The *múlo* then cooks her to dissolve her bones so that she may become his wife. To prevent this the Gypsies strew seeds of the jimson weed, the witch's herb, beneath their beds. If datura seeds are cast on a *múlo*, it will flee.

At Christmas, a time when the *múlo* is invisible, it will come and sit on a kind of stretcher that the men carry around the church three times to obtain riches. This makes the stretcher so heavy that its bearers can no longer move forward, and they are slain by the *múlos*. To avoid this misfortune a man will continuously sweep the stretcher with a piece of new linen so that these demons will be unable to sit on it. A more effective method is as follows: On one of the three nights of Christmas, the most recently deceased person is disinterred and his corpse is dragged around the church three times. Only two men should be present: the one dragging the cadaver and the other who strikes it with a willow branch that has three "eyes" (*yakhori*)—three buds—on its upper end so that the soul will disconnect itself (*jipen the prejial*). But this procedure is dangerous, because the soul of the dead person can enter one of these two men. If the soul succeeds, these men will be able to see the hidden treasures every night, but they will remain possessed.

During Christmas week the *múlos* celebrate their annual festival and attack women. To protect themselves the women hang a clove of nutmeg and a little camphor in a handkerchief in front of their caves.

To prevent a child who died before being baptized from transforming into a *múlo* it is necessary to pour water, which was collected from beneath the rain gutter of a church, on the child's grave for nine nights in a row under a waning moon. People also place peas in the dead child's grave. But if someone goes to the home of the *múlos* and eats a piece of his dead child, the child will emerge from the cauldron alive—it will only be missing the piece that its father ate.

There are two curiosities relating to the *múlo* that should also be mentioned. In one Gypsy prayer the *múlo* takes the place of the Holy Ghost in the Trinity (*devleskore múlo*), and in the "Lenore" type of ballad, which recounts the return of the dead fiancé, the revenant is a *múlo*. The finest examples of the latter type of tale can be found in the Greek Acritic songs and in the Czech literary classic *Kytice* [A Bouquet of Folk Legends] by Karel Jaromír Erben.

📖 Wlislocki, *Volksdichtungen*, 104–6, 245–49; Wlislocki, *Vom wandernden Zigeunervolke*, 93–95, 148–49, 298; Ville, *Tsiganes,* 116; Martinez, "Du 'mulo' tsigane au 'mujao' andalou"; Erdös, "La notion de *mulo* ou mort-vivant et le culte des morts chez les Tsiganes hongrois"; Knobloch, "Gypsy Tales concerning the 'Mulo.'"

MULTIHEADED MAN: There is a story in Transylvania that tells how a man with five heads came out of the forest on the day of Easter and surprised the Gypsy Radulf Pišta who was foraging for food. The five-headed man reproached him for this, but the Gypsy argued that he had fifteen children to feed, seven of whom were blind and seven of whom were deaf. After receiving confirmation from Pišta's wife that what he had said was true, the stranger from the forest asked that the fifteenth child, who was neither deaf nor blind, be sacrificed to him, and the child was cast out the window. The seven deaf children could hear their brother weeping in the street, and the seven blind children ran out and could see that he was safe and sound. The motif of multiheaded men is so rare in European folklore that researchers believe that this story most likely originated in India (cf. the god Shiva).

📖 Wlislocki, *Märchen und Sagen,* no. 31.

MYTHIC COSMOGRAPHY: The sky is an empty space, above which remains the Old Man (*pçuro manuš*); that is to say, the heavens, personified as Čero, who is the husband of the Earth (Pçuv, Phuv). According to one Serbian tradition the world is borne on the horns of a giant ox who causes earthquakes whenever he twitches his ears. The Gypsies believe that the Earth will be destroyed on the day when he shakes his head. This tradition corresponds to the belief found among several tribal groups in northwest India and Pakistan: the Gond, the Bhil, and the Kanjar.

✦ *Earth, Ox, Sky*

📖 Wlislocki, *Aus dem inneren Leben,* 60; Berger, "Mythologie der Zigeuner," 794 (with bibliography).

NEGRO: One day God took some flour and water and used it to make some little men. He put them in the oven. His first attempt created people with black skin color because he overcooked the dough.

📖 Jangil, *Voyage maison,* 77–78; Leland, *The English Gipsies and Their Language,* 319; Kabakova and Stroeva, *Contes et Légendes tsiganes,* 21; Groome, *Gypsies, Tinkers and Other Travellers,* 145.

NETCHAPHORO: This is the name of the star that appeared in the sky (*nébos*) when the "little God" (Jesus) was born. When the Jews saw this star they slew their own children, causing all their stars to fall from the heavens, leaving the star of the Son of God alone in the sky. It is believed that the source of this story is the *Infancy Gospel of James,* an apocryphal text that is widespread in the Eastern Church.

✦ *Gospel of the Gypsies*

Netchaphoro/tchalai tschernia: Star

NETTLE (*çadcerli*): Nettles grow most profusely where an underground passage leads to the dwelling of a *phuvuš,* and they are therefore made sacred by him. They are called *Kásta Pçuvasengré* ("Wood, or forest, of the *phuvuš*").

✦ *Pçuvuš*

📖 Wlislocki, *Volksleben,* 93; Leland, *The English Gipsies and Their Language,* 96.

NICHOLAS (Saint): He appears in Gypsy stories in the form of an old man or an old beggar who comes to the aid of people who deserve it. He owns a wondrous bird with a red head, white feet, and golden wings who procures food and drink for its owner but disappears when the owner dies. To reward a young man who provided him with shelter while he was ill, Nicholas offered the man a wooden bird that would fly once he had been seated on its back. Thanks to this unique flying creature the young man managed to wed a reclusive princess.

Saint Nicholas punished a Bohemian who mistreated him by throwing the man up to the moon. The saint went on to tell him: "Know that I am Saint Nicholas and that on the evening of the Nativity, I would have given you so much money you would have become richer than the earl who dwells high above in a castle. He lodged and fed me, a poor devil, for three days and nights, without driving me away or demanding money. This is why he will be even richer and happier. As for you, you are going to also receive your just reward: you will have to live on the moon and eat it." This is the origin of the phases of the moon.

📖 Wlislocki, *Märchen und Sagen,* nos. 6, 53; Wlislocki, *Volksdichtungen,* no. 66.

NIVAŠI/NIVASHI (pl. *nivašá, niváshá*): These are water spirits who live in golden houses located at the bottom of lakes. The males have puffed up bodies, horses' hooves, and red hair and beards. They are sometimes quite hairy. Their hands are moist and icy cold. They visit women while they are sleeping, after which the women carry a serpent inside them. They turn them into sorceresses, "good ladies" (*lace romñi*), or even "wisewomen" (*gule romñi*), to whom they teach the secrets of healing and to whom they bring all the plants that bolts of lightning have stolen away from the Tree of All Seeds. When a man crosses over a bridge they will drag him into the water if they can and drown him. They then imprison his soul inside a pot and take a keen delight in listening to its wailing. They will not let it go until the cadaver has rotted away. They like to change themselves into quail (*bereçto; firyo; ciriklo bengeskro,* the "Devil's bird") and spend their days in the fields before stealing the grain at night. They are friendly to humans and pile them high with gifts when a young woman who has fallen into the water lives with them, but she can live no more than a day. They possess a golden egg that will transform any metal it touches into gold, but only its legitimate owner can profit from this capability.

When a *nivaši* grows old his fellow *nivašá* will eat him. "Nivaši" is also given as the name of the king of the *prikulič.* They live beneath water in a glass palace in which they keep the souls of the drowned in black barrels.

The *nivaši* women are extremely beautiful with eyes that shine like stars. They have very thick hair that serves them as a garment, or else they wear clothes that are as white as snow, and red shoes. They live in splendid palaces where they bring the mortals with whom they have fallen in love. Their firstborn offspring does not have any bones (*bikokalengéro*), but is able to walk and swim at birth, and becomes a *nivaši;* it brings bad luck and only stays on land for thirty years, then returns to the waters. After this the *nivaši* can only give birth to two daughters. She and her husband will then die, and the devil will carry them away.

When a *nivaši* falls in love with a man she will embrace him

Nivaši

with her arms that are as cold as ice, but she gradually warms up. She will bring him underwater to her palace that sparkles with gold and silver and return him to his people every nine days and fill his pockets with gold. If her husband seeks to marry a human woman, however, he will be drowned by the sons whom he had with the *nivaši.*

When a *nivaši* is dancing in the moonlight, if a young mortal manages to prevent her from fleeing—either by means of datura seeds or by taking her red shoes—he will win a loyal wife for his entire life. A drop of blood from the left hand of a *nivaši* will cure blindness. When a Gypsy has a skin rash he lets a few drops of blood from his ring finger fall in to running water before the sun rises; if a *nivaši* drinks it, he will be cured.

If a Gypsy is suffering from dropsy he will go to some running water when the moon is waning and let a few drops of blood from his index finger fall in to it so that the *nivaši* will "draw" the excess fluid from his body. When he cuts his index finger (*sikájimáko*) he should take care to let none of the blood fall on the ground, otherwise the *nivaša* will take it and he will be drowned sooner or later. In southern Hungary, when a child is crying uncontrollably, its mother will make the child walk around the fire three times, wash its head with water in which she has placed three coals, and then go to the nearest place with running water. There she will toss a red string into the water while saying, "*Nivaši* take this string and with it the tears of my child! When he is better, I will bring you apples and eggs!" (*Lává Nivaši ádá bolditori te láhá m're čaveskro rovipen! Káná sástavestes ánáv me tute pçábáyá te yándrá!*) This offering is frequently cited in the folklore accounts.

Researchers have noted the kinship between the *nivaša* and the *Ashvins,* the celestial physicians from Indian mythology who sometimes have the form of horses.

The *nivaši* and the *phuvuš* are often associated with one another in the charms for ensuring a good birth. Charms are also used to protect the domestic animals from the *nivašá,* but they are primarily invoked to recover livestock that has been stolen and to fight worms, especially those involved in skin diseases.

✦ *Datura, Pçuvuš, Prikulič, Tree of All Seeds*

📖 Wlislocki, *Aus dem inneren Leben*, 3, 136; Wlislocki, *Vom wandernden Zigeunervolke*, 181, 229–30, 238, 372–77; Wlislocki, *Volksglaube*, 57–58, 135; Wlislocki, *Volksdichtungen*, nos. 21, 22, 23, 24; Wlislocki, *Märchen und Sagen*, nos. 24, 36; Leland, *Gypsy Sorcery and Fortune Telling*, 60, 81, 110.

NOON (*mitago, mitageskro, dýlos*): This is the hour of King Sun, and it is also the moment when there is communication between paradise (*rayo*) and hell (*yado*), which also permits the *múlo* to find passage into our world.

✦ *King Sun, Múlo, Rayo, Yado*

📖 Jangil, *Voyage maison*, 62.

OGRE, OGRESS: ✦ Curko, Dragon

OLD WOMAN (THE): This is a straw mannequin dressed like a woman to represent the Queen of Shadows, who brings illness, famine, and death before she vanishes at the onset of spring. This effigy is placed upon a beam where people strike it with clubs before sawing it in half. It is then burned in to ashes that are cast into a body of running water. This is easily recognizable as a rite for driving away winter. Such rites are common throughout Europe and occur in a variety of forms.

✦ *Queen of Shadows*

ORIOLE: This is believed to be a young woman who has been metamorphosed into this bird. An oriole asks a Gypsy to help her at the moment its song is at its most beautiful. A gold marble then falls from her beak. This is her enchanted heart and the source of her song. The marble grants the power to guess the thoughts of others, and in one tale this is how the hero vanquishes a dragon. He then returns to the spot where he had encountered the oriole and finds a beautiful princess there, but she has no heart. The Gypsy gives her back her marble, she swallows it, and thus regains her heart once more.

📖 Ficowski, *Le Rameau de l'arbre,* 57–61.

OTHER WORLD (THE), THE KINGDOM OF THE
DEAD: The land of the dead is located on a mountain, in a cave or inside a hollow mountain, where it is guarded by nine white dogs. The Gypsies of Transylvania have a custom of letting dogs of that color lick people when they are on their deathbeds. Once the body of the deceased has rotted away he will struggle to make his way to the Other World. This is a painful and terrible journey that takes nine years. He must travel close to seven mountains that fight one another (which is reminiscent of the clashing rocks in Ancient Greek myth, the Symplegades) and confront a snake who blocks the road and demands milk and honey in return for allowing him to pass. He must have meat to give to the nine dogs and cross through a dozen deserts that are swept by a glacial wind that is as sharp as a knife. This is the reason why his relatives burn his clothing and bedding: to give him warmth. They also give him milk for this journey, otherwise the dead individual will remain trapped between the two worlds. Once the individual has reached his destination he or she continues to lead a life corresponding to the one they led while still alive: a blind man will remain blind, for example, and a cripple will remain crippled. But the individual cannot reach the Other World if his or her body has not been washed, nor will this destination be accessible if the hairs weren't burned and the nails not cut while still alive. On the other hand, magicians that feel the approach of death will allow the nails on their hands and feet to grow so that they will be able to scale the sides of the mountains.

A curious tale recounts how a little child died shortly after his baptism but was unable to enter the kingdom of the dead for he had not yet paid for the suffering that his birth had inflicted on his mother. When he got there the wind froze him, and he was sent back to Earth to make a fire. On his second attempt he came across a serpent who demanded that he give him honey and milk to let him pass. And on his last attempt he ran in to nine white dogs who clamored for meat. Once he had satisfied their requests, "they allowed him to enter the kingdom of the dead forever."

The souls of stillborn children are carried about in a large sack by an old woman. Time passes by very swiftly in the empire of the dead.

📖 Wlislocki, *Vom wandernden Zigeunervolke*, 145–47, 300–304; Wlislocki, *Zur Volkskunde* (1887), 29–35; Wlislocki, *Märchen und Sagen*, no. 25; Wlislocki, *Volksdichtungen*, no. 41; Wlislocki, *Aus dem inneren Leben*, 280; Wlislocki, "Gebräuche der transsilvanischen Zeltzigeuner," 269; *Zanko, chef tribal chez les Chalderash*, 95–103.

OWL (*uvika, ratjakro, čiriklo*): The Gypsies believe that a worm (*kirmo*), the worm of good fortune, can be found in the egg of the owl.

📖 Wlislocki, *Volksdichtungen*, 307.

OX (*guruv, guru*): A story that is connected to the tale of the Tree of All Seeds (*Save sumbreskro kasht*) tells of the sacrifice of an ox to a river spirit on the first day of the new year. When this ritual ceased to be upheld in the wake of bad advice from a foreigner who was black as soot, all the plant life died, and famine

struck the land. The spirit of the waters appeared to a holy man in the form of an old man, gave him seeds that would allow all the plant life to be restored, and strongly urged that the custom of the sacrifice be faithfully implemented once again.

The Gypsies of Serbia believe that the world rests upon the horns of an ox; when the animal flicks his ears, the whole world trembles, and on the day when he shakes his entire head, the world will disappear.

✦ *Tree of All Seeds*

📖 Berger, "Mythologie der Zigeuner," 794.

PANI: He is the master of the waters. In certain Balkan regions he is depicted as a hybrid being that resembles a kind of aquatic satyr. His name is related to the Sanskrit word *pānīya,* "water."

PANTHEON: The gods are ruled by Devla (from the Sanskrit *deva,* "god"), who is represented as a creator and the Father of the Sky, whereas Beng (Bengi, Bang), who went on to become the devil, rules over the Earth and lives underground. His spirits are called Bengesko, while those of Devla are called Develeski and are the equivalent of angels. They are reminiscent of the Indian Devas. They are followed by the Earth Mother, Phuri Dai; Sun and Moon; the personified elements Fire (Yag) and Wind (Bavol), born of the coupling of the Sky and the Earth; and Rom, the great ancestor of the Gypsies, who is sometimes conflated with Cain or Tubalcain and regarded as the child of Adam and Lilith or of Cain and Eve.

In the lower echelon of the pantheon we find the demons of the wind (*bavolshi*), of fire and lightning (*yagshi*), of water (*nivashi, panishi*), and of the earth (*phuvushi*).

PATRON OF JOURNEYS: This figure appears in the form of a serpent or an old man who defines himself as follows: "I am the patron of journeys, patron of the flights of birds and of Gypsy wanderings. I help the Gypsies and the birds." In one tale he comes to the aid of a young man who refused to cage his winged charges and gives him a splendid fledgling with a red head, white feet, and black wings who would grant all his wishes except those involving dishonesty or misappropriation.

✦ *Serpent*

📖 Ficowski, *Le Rameau de l'arbre*, 183.

PÇUVUŠ, PHUVUSH (fem. *pçuvuši;* pl. *pçuvsheyá*): The *pçuvuš* is a small, ugly, and hairy chthonic spirit who dwells under the ground. Sometimes it is described as looking like a mole with a human head. Its name is a compound of *pçuv,* "earth," and *manuš,* "man." The English Gypsies call this spirit *poovus.* It possesses three hairs of gold that make it invisible when above ground, but if it dons a cap it will become visible. If a person manages to tear out one of this spirit's hairs, he or she will become wealthy as every stone they touch with the hair will be transformed in to gold. The *pçuvuš* keeps under guard a black hen who conceals three eggs: one is red, one is white, and the third is black. This latter egg holds the spirit's strength, and if anyone were to toss it into the water the *pçuvuš* would be slain. The white egg emits light and shows the path leading out of the spirit's cave, and the red egg will open the door that seals the cavern.

The *pçuvuš* is generally kindhearted but will abduct women. Its life (external soul), or strength, as noted earlier, is hidden in a black egg of a black hen, which if ever cast into water will not only slay the *pçuvuš* but also cause an earthquake. In Transylvania and the Banat region such an earthquake is called *meriben pçuvušeskro,* "the death of the *pçuvuš*." When the *pçuvuš* travels aboveground he carries two other eggs: the white one rolls in front of him and illuminates his path; the red one is needed to roll aside the boulder that seals the entrance to his subterranean

Pçuvuš

kingdom. The Gypsies believe that these chthonic spirits are the sworn enemies of all kinds of worms and crawling insects, with the exception of the snail, which is called the "horse of the *pçuvuš*" (*gráy pçuvuš engré*).

When an infant refuses to breastfeed the Gypsies believe this is evidence that a *pçuvuši* or another chthonic spirit has already nursed it. In these cases they place onions between the mother's breasts and pronounce a charm intended to make the spirit ill (*Pçuvuši, Pçuvuši / Ac tu nášvályi . . .*). The *pçuvuš* is also invoked by the Gypsies of southern Hungary to prevent thefts and to stop nosebleeds. It is likewise invoked when lighting a fire in front of the tent of a pregnant woman who is feeling her first labor pains.

> *Eitrá Pçuvušá, efta Nivášyá*
> *André mal avená*
> *Pçabuven, pçabuven, oh yákhá!*
> *Dáyákri punro dindálen,*
> *Te gule čaves mudáren*

Pçabuven, pçabuven, oh yákhá;
Ferinen o čaves te daya!

Seven *pçuvuša,* seven *nivašya*
Are coming by way of the field
Fire, grab them!
They want to bite the mother's leg,
Want to kill her little child;
Fire, fire, burn quick;
Save the mother, save the child!

People also turn to the *pçuvuš* when they are having eye problems.

Oh dukh ándrál yákhá
Já ándré páñi
Já andrál páñi,
Andre safráne
André pçuv.
Já andrál pçuv.
Kiyá Pçuvusheske.
Odoy hin cerçá!
Odoyjateça!

O pains of my eyes
Pass into the water,
From water into saffron,
From saffron
Into the ground.
To the home of the pçuvuš.
There is where you dwell.
Go there and eat!
Go there and eat!

This spirit is also invoked for healing swollen testicles and for various forms of rheumatism.

Wasps and bumblebees are considered to be the companions of the *pçuvuša;* they should not be allowed to come indoors for they will bring discord. If ever you find a wasp nest, you are sure to meet a person who wishes you ill. The green woodpecker and the bullfinch are the favorite birds of the *pçuvuša.* Wherever one of these birds can be heard, you can be certain that a *pçuvuš* is lurking nearby. These chthonic spirits sometimes stroll aboveground, making sure they remain invisible by leaving their three gold hairs uncovered. The green woodpecker and the bullfinch will send them a signal, and, depending on what the *pçuvuš* wishes, he will cover these three gold hairs or leave them exposed.

The *pçuvuš* is equated with the devil in the expression "go out of the ground and go to the *pçuvuš.*" This phrase forms part of a charm against eye problems.

According to one legend a *pçuvuš* played a key role in the origin of the Kukuya tribe. In some of the folktales he will help humans but will demand a girl in return; in other tales he buys brooms from a Bohemian and makes him wealthy. A *pçuvuši* numb from the cold is warmed by the fire made by a young man, whom she rewards with coals that are as cold as ice but that turn in to gold.

Ficowski, *Le Rameau de l'arbre,* 71; Wlislocki, *Volksdichtungen,* nos. 14–18, 42; Wlislocki, *Aus dem inneren Leben,* 3, 165; Wlislocki, *Volksglaube,* 157–58, 168; Leland, *Gypsy Sorcery and Fortune Telling,* 27–28, 46–48, 59–60, 96–97.

PHALLUS (*kar*): A phallus that has been carved out of blackthorn and kept in the house will banish misfortune; in the event of danger, prayers are made to it. Among the Gypsies and Slavs of the South, a nail takes the place of the phallus. In Hungary a bride would secretly stick a nail into her future marriage bed to increase the sexual potency of her husband (*manusheskro sor bárvalyol*).

📖 Berger, "Mythologie der Zigeuner," 804; Wlislocki, *Volksglaube,* 106.

PHARAVONO (Pharaoh): This figure is part of the Gypsies' legend of their Egyptian origin, which can be found throughout the tribes of Eastern Europe. Gypsies are the Egyptians that escaped drowning in the waves of the Red Sea. Zanko, the tribal leader of the Kalderash, essentially recounts the following: Originally Pharavono was the chief of the Pharavunure and one of the saints who comprise the ancestors of humanity. He waged war against the other tribes—the Horachai, "the Turco-Jews, and the Christians," who were led by Sinpetra—to wrest the Holy Land from them. Pharavono shot an arrow above the river to find out if he could cross it, but it was too wide. Pharavono then spoke a spell: "By the power of Del (God), for me! By the strength of God, for my horses!" but he was unaware that his adversary was God the Father. He crossed the river, and Sinpetra retreated across the salty sea. When he reached the shores of this body of water Pharavono repeated his spell, and Sinpetra made him a path through the sea. But when he and his army began marching across, God folded his arms and the sea closed back up, swallowing the Pharavunure. From amid the waves Pharavono raised his arms in the direction of a stone idol that was in a cave on Sinpetra's shore. He cast a lightning bolt that destroyed the idol. The few Pharavunure who survived went to Zagreb, from where they spread to the rest of the world. It is quite easy to recognize the crossing of the Red Sea from the Bible (Exodus 2:14) in this legendary account. But the Gypsies no longer had anything—no territory, no political organization, no church, nor an alphabet—because the sea had swept away their entire culture.

✦ *Kakava, Sinpetra*

📖 Berger, "Mythologie der Zigeuner," 804–5; *Zanko, chef tribal chez les Chalderash,* 28–35.

PHIRAUN: This is the Muslim form of "Pharaoh." Phiraun lives in a high tower so that he will be like God. He produces thunder by using drums, and he creates rain by pouring water through a sieve.

  📖 Berger, "Mythologie der Zigeuner," 805.

PHUVUSH: ✦ Pçuvuš

PIGEON (*pinsteri, tojba, tovadri, pennistehra*): According to the Gypsy traditions, every pigeon will, at one time in its life, go hunt for food in the Tree of All Seeds, whose leaves are silver and gold.

  📖 Wlislocki, *Vom wandernden Zigeunervolke,* 127; Wlislocki, *Märchen und Sagen,* nos. 10, 11, 15, 16, 24, 42, 48; Wlislocki, *Volksdichtungen,* nos. 20, 24.

PORESKORO ("the Tailed One"): This is the ninth and last child of Ana, the queen of the *kešalyia.* He has four cat heads, four more dog heads, the body of a bird, and a serpent's tail.

Poreskoro

He is linked to plague and cholera. The following legend explains his origin. Seeing that the queen was sad because she had to marry the king of the *loçolicos,* the *kešalyia* decided to come to her aid. They took some hairs from the dogs who guard the kingdom of the dead and mixed them with powdered serpent and cat fur to make a cake that they gave to Ana's husband to eat, and he fathered Poreskoro. A person whom Poreskoro touches with the first of his four dog heads will die, and someone who is licked by the first of his four cat heads will never recover their health.

✦ *Kešalyia, Loçolicos*

📖 Wlislocki, *Aus dem inneren Leben,* 26–27.

PRIKULIČ: Although for the Transylvanian Gypsies in Central Europe the *prikulič* is thought to be a revenant, a kind of vampire, for others it is a spirit who lives in marshes and caverns or a water spirit subject to a *nivaši.* He bought the girl with the golden hair and forced her to spin thread from her hair to make a cloth. To force them to speak and thereby prevent her from being freed, he tortured her would-be rescuers.

📖 Wlislocki, *Märchen und Sagen,* 77–78, 90–91; Wlislocki, "Quälgeister im Volksglauben der Rumänen," 17–19.

PROROC AND ILIA: These are two mythical heroes whose story Zanko, the tribal leader of the Kalderash, told to the Reverend Father Chatard.

The devils duped a peasant by the name of Ilia by making him believe that his wife was cheating on him in his absence. When he returned home, where all was dark, he killed the couple he found laying together in the vestibule but learned to his horror that he had just murdered his parents. While he was weeping over their death with his wife, some doves knocked at the window and advised him to take some of their plumage and pass the feathers over the bodies of the deceased. His parents came back to life. The father, Proroc, granted his son Ilia's request for a spear and lightning to drive the devils (*beńga*) away. He pursued them on land and in the air, and every time he slew one miscarriages and conflagrations would occur on the Earth. To put an end to the furious madness of his son, Proroc, on the advice of his wife, arranged matters so that Ilia would lose an arm and a leg, but it was only after he lost an eye too that the balance of the world was restored, even though Ilia continued his hunt of the demons.

It has been suggested that this legend was borrowed from the bylina [a traditional form of Old Russian epic oral poetry —*Trans.*] about the hero Ilya Muromets. In the bylina, however, the role of the devils is played by Tatars, and thus the narrative lacks the cosmic dimension of the Gypsy legend.

 📖 *Zanko, chef tribal chez les Chalderash,* 95–103; Berger, "Mythologie der Zigeuner," 807; Gruel-Apert, *Le Monde mythologique russe,* 193–96.

PUMPKIN (*dudum*): In the legend about the origin of the *múlo* (a kind of vampire) an old man advises a woman who wishes to have a child to fashion a bowl out of a pumpkin, fill it with water, and drink it under the waxing moon. The woman follows these instructions and gives birth to a child who dies nine months later. Her husband visits the home of the *múlo,* and one of these vampire-like creatures makes him eat the flesh of his child who has been cooked in a cauldron. Then he pulls the little child from the cauldron and gives it back to his father.

 ✦ *Múlo*

 📖 Wlislocki, *Vom wandernden Zigeunervolke,* 93–94.

QUAIL (*bereçto, füryo, wachtla*): The Gypsies call the quail the "devil's bird" (*ciriclo bengeskro*) and attribute diabolical features to it. During the day the *nivášyá* appear in the form of this bird in the fields, and at night they steal the grain. To prevent them from doing this, pieces of quail are placed at the four corners of the field, or if these are not available, feathers from a black hen who has never laid an egg are used.

In one tale God transformed two young people into quail because they successively denied bread to an old woman, an old man, and a child. The two became lovers and condemned their offspring to live in the fields, where they had to painfully seek out enough food upon which to live.

📖 Groome, *Gypsy Folk-Tales,* 89; Leland, *Gypsy Sorcery and Fortune Telling,* 87–90; Wlislocki, *Volksdichtungen,* no. 10.

QUEEN OF THE SHADOWS (*ushalyakri thagari*): This figure appears at the onset of winter to bring illness, famine, and death to humanity, and she vanishes in the spring. She is represented by a straw mannequin dressed like a woman, and she is called "the Old Woman." On the afternoon of the "Day of the Shadows" (*ushalyakri jives*), the last Sunday before Easter, in the square, she is placed on a beam and the people who are present hit her with cudgels. It is then sawed in half—which is called "sawing the Old Woman" (*pçures yon cinen*)—by a young man and a young woman, both of whom are disguised. The mannequin is then burned, and its ashes are thrown in a waterway. Among the Hungarian Gypsies this mannequin is represented as a sacrifice offered to the Queen of Shadows for having spared the folk over the winter. Among the Transylvanian Gypsies the mannequin is clad in the worn-out clothing of the most recently widowed woman. She is happy to contribute the clothes for this purpose, because she views their incineration as a greeting to her late husband, who is thereby compelled to remain in the kingdom of the dead and can no longer come visit her.

📖 Wlislocki, *Volksglaube,* 145–46.

QUEEN OF THE SNOW: This is a daughter or the wife of King Mist.

✦ *King Mist*

RAINBOW (*kchérmisa, stafelyi*): This natural phenomenon permits a person to climb up to the sky and obtain eternal health and beauty, but its end has to be found on the day of Pentecost. It is a good idea at that time to stick a knife in the ground at this location and leave it there until the rainbow disappears. This knife will give its user the power to cut the "worm of madness" beneath the tongues of animals that have gone berserk.

It is believed that a child will become extraordinarily beautiful or handsome if the end of a rainbow passes over it.

📖 Wlislocki, *Vom wandernden Zigeunervolke*, 161; Wlislocki, *Volksdichtungen*, 54.

RAYO, RAIIO: This is the name of paradise, the place where the good human beings go after death to rejoin Sinpetra.

📖 Jangil, *Voyage maison*, 79.

REGINA SOLEIKA: This is the name of the queen mother of all the Zingali. They rejoin her after death.

✦ *Death*

RESURRECTION: There are a variety of texts that attest to the Gypsy belief in metempsychosis. A young man is killed and buried

by his brothers. A willow grows over his grave, and the father of
the deceased man takes some of its slender branches to make a
flute. When he plays it, it speaks to him and reveals the murder. It
then spells out these instructions:

> Burn half the large claw of the *chagrin* [*ḫágrin*],
> Cover me with its ashes
> And you shall bring me back to life.

Other methods relate to cutting the body into pieces.

✦ *Dismemberment*

📖 Wlislocki, *Volksdichtungen*, no. 32.

REVENANT (*múlo*): If certain rites are not respected the dead
will come back or they will be unable to make their way to the
Other World.

To prevent the return of the dead the cadaver is washed with
salty water, then it is dressed and removed from the tent or cabin
through the east side. The body is then placed on the ground
with its head next to a stake that is struck with several of the
deceased's favorite objects (violin, pipe, and so forth) while the
corpse is asked: "Are you dead because the great God wished it?"
If the body does not move closer to the stake the answer is yes
and indicates a natural death. If the opposite occurs people set
off in pursuit of the murderer. All of the deceased's property is
removed so that his soul will not bump in to it, which would
provoke his vengeance.

During the vigil people drink brandy (*Tatti-pāni*), sing, and
dance. They weep and moan around the cadaver to the point of
exhaustion, for it is believed that all this will prevent the soul
from returning to the body before it is buried. If this is not done
the deceased will not enjoy rest and will often come back and
cause problems.

During the funeral feast people will occasionally drop a crumb of food and a drop of their drink for the soul fluttering around the body to ingest in secret. The Gypsies of Transylvania place a bowl of milk next to the cadaver so that the soul can strengthen itself before undertaking its journey into the Beyond.

The dead individual is buried in a remote corner of the village cemetery or at the edge of the forest, and the grave is marked with a wedge-shaped stick, the top end of which barely protrudes above the surface of the ground and the bottom end of which touches the head of the deceased. Sometimes thorn bushes are planted at the location "so that no stranger can walk over the grave."

If an infant dies before being baptized or has entered the world stillborn, the grave will be sprinkled with the mother's milk, and peas will be cast around it to prevent the infant's return. The infant's grave is also watered with the water from the church rain gutter to prevent its return as a vampire.

✦ *Dead (The), Soul*

📖 Wlislocki, *Märchen und Sagen*, no. 25; Wlislocki, *Vom wandernden Zigeunervolke*, 93.

ROM (fem. *romni*): They are the first men, the direct descendants of Adam and Eve (Damo and Yehwah). They were of one race, and it was as a single people that they became nomads with Sinpetra. Then the Sunts ("the ancestors") came, accompanied by Pharavono, who would later be responsible for the division of humanity into two groups: the Horaxané, led by Sinpetra; and the Pharavonure, led by Pharavono.

"Rom" is related to the Sanskrit *rama*, "husband, spouse," as well as to Rama, one of the incarnations of Vishnu.

✦ *Anthropogeny, Egyptian, Gypsy, Pharavono, Sinpetra*

📖 Jangil, *Voyage maison*, 80.

ROSE (*rosa, sungemaskri*): The Gypsies explain the origin of this flower with the following tale. Due to the slanderous things his relatives were telling him, a young man killed his wife because he thought she was cheating on him. He then ripped out her heart and burned it outdoors before running away to the mountains where he perished miserably. Out of the ashes a bush sprouted with red roses, born from his wife's heart. His perfidious relatives were changed in to thorns and stuck onto the bush.

📖 Wlislocki, *Volksdichtungen,* no. 8.

SAINT JOHN'S NIGHT: This is the date on which all the supernatural beings can visit humans, either to help or harm them. If a person climbs one of the Blessed Mountains on this night he or she will have the place and circumstances of their death revealed through a dream. On this night it is a good idea to leave a pot of milk in front of one's tent so that the dead who are unable to find rest in the ground can obtain relief from the fatigue brought on by their wanderings. The Transylvanian nomads stretch a white string over the running waters so that the souls of the dead who have not yet made their way to the Other World will be able to cross them, because water has, since time immemorial, represented the border between life and death. On Saint John's Night only the ninth son of a family in which no daughter has been born to break the succession of the brothers, can see these souls in their human form.

On St. John's Night the fairies (Urme) come to announce the fate of newborns and grant them gifts.

✦ *Blessed Mountains, Urme*

📖 Wlislocki, *Volksdichtungen,* nos. 46, 47; Wlislocki, *Aus dem inneren Leben,* 57; Wlislocki, *Volksglaube,* 158; Wlislocki, "Gebräuche der transsilvanischen Zigeuner," 270.

SARAH THE BLACK (*Sara e Káli*): She was the first woman to receive the Revelation. The Roma were polytheistic and carried the statue of Ishtari (Astarte) in a procession down to the sea to be blessed. One night Sarah had a vision that informed her that some saints who had been present at the death of Jesus were coming and that they would need her aid. Sarah saw them approaching the shore in a boat that the rough seas were threatening to capsize. She spread her robe over the waves and, using it like a raft, sailed it out to the saints and helped them to reach land.

Sarah is worshipped at Saintes-Maries-de-la-Mer.

Sarah is the saint who is worshipped at Saintes-Maries-de-la-Mer in southern France. It is believed she may represent a Christianized form of Kali, the Indian goddess of fate and good fortune.

📖 Buckland, *Book of Gypsy Magic,* 144; Delage, "Les Saintes-Maries-de-la-Mer"; Bloch, *Les Tsiganes,* 78–80; Berge, "Les Bohémiens-Caraques et leur Terre Sainte de Camargue."

SATAN: ✦ Devil

ŠERKANO: ✦ King Serpent

ŠILÁLYI/SHILALI ("the Cold One," "the Fever"): This is the fifth child and the third daughter of Ana and the king of the *loçolicos.*

Shilali

She takes the form of a small mouse (*múša*) endowed with a great number of feet. She is the cause of cold fever. It is said that she was born from Ana's mouth. Melálo, the eldest son, wanted to have a sister and asked his father to take a mouse, spit on it, and then put it in his wife's soup. His father did this, and his child got his wish. Ana ate the soup, fell ill and asked for water, and at the very moment she did this a mouse who had thousands of feet scampered out of her mouth. Ana was gripped by fever. The mouse ran up and down her body, which began shivering with cold. Ana cursed the new child and gave her the name of Šilályi.

Charles G. Leland has collected several charms for curing

fever (*šilályi*), which banish the disease into the water or a tree (*transplantatio morbi*), such as the following:

> *Shilályi prejiá,*
> *Páñori me tut 'dáv!*
> *Andakode prejiá,*
> *Náñi me tut kámáv,*
> *Odoy tut čučiden,*
> *Odoy tut ferinen,*
> *Odoy tut may kámen!*
> *Mashurdalo sástyár!*

> Fever, go far away from me,
> Water, I give it to you!
> You are not dear to me,
> So get out of here,
> Return whence you came,
> There where someone gives you shelter,
> There where someone loves you!
> Mashurdalo, help!

✦ *Ana, Loçolico, Melálo*

📖 Wlislocki, *Aus dem inneren Leben,* 15–20; Leland, *Gypsy Sorcery and Fortune Telling,* 16–19.

SINPETRA: According to Zanko, the tribal leader of the Kalderash, Sinpetra is the name of the "great God" (*phuro del*). Originally Sinpetra was a giant who created the first and second worlds, as well as the first human couple. His companions were the saints Avraham, Moses, Cretchuno (Joseph), Yacchof (Jacob), and Moishel, "the great ancestors of all men." His son is called *sunto del,* "holy God," or *amaro del,* "our God."

But Sinpetro is also Saint Peter, who has been conflated with the figure of God.

📖 *Zanko, chef tribal chez les Chalderash,* 35–36.

SKY (*niebos, nebos, eros/tscherosz*): The Gypsy conception of the sky views it as a tree bearing golden apples. One day when a child was gravely ill he asked his father to give him a star to eat so he could regain his health, but his father responded: "Alas, the tree of heaven is very tall and I am not able to grab any of them, but pray to God to keep you alive until the sky rots and turns upside down. Then you will be able to cook yourself two stars."

Another word, *Praio,* defines the sky simply as a "higher country."

📖 Haltrich, *Zur Volkkunde der siebenbürgischen Sachsen,* 114.

SMITH: ✦ Daud Alayes Salaam

SNAIL (*buvero, sneko*): The Gypsies believe that the *phuvuš* are the sworn enemies of worms and other animals who crawl or slither, except for the snail, which they call the "Horse of the *phuvuš*" (*Gray phuvuš engré*). The shells of snails are believed to transform in to golden eggs a year later and to bring luck to whoever finds them.

✦ *Pçuvuš*

📖 Wlislocki, *Vom wandernden Zigeunervolke,* 130, 213; Wlislocki, *Volksdichtungen,* 95.

SNAKE (sg. *sarp, sap;* pl. *sappors;* diminutive *sápóro*): The Gypsies consider the snake to be a sacred animal. Even today in the spring the Kalderash celebrate "the day of the divine serpent"; this serpent possesses several features of a god of meteors, from whom thunder and lightning emanate. Zanko tells the following story, which I will summarize here.

While nursing on his mother, Stoika, Potro bit her breasts and she cursed him, condemning him when he reached the age of twenty to be swallowed by the "hundred-year-old serpent" and to remain inside his belly for forty days. When Potro turned twenty years old he went to see the snake in the forest. The serpent swallowed him feet first, until only his head was sticking out of his mouth. Forty days later Potro's grandfather arrived to free him by slitting open the stomach of the reptile.* The Gypsy tribunal condemned the mother to be tied to the tail of a horse and dragged along the ground until dead. Soon all that was left of her was her head with its eyes wide open.

A snake holds in its mouth the roots—or, according to one tale, the crown—of the Tree of All Seeds. It is also a reptile who holds back the giant attached to a boulder.

A good demon who is the patron of Gypsy travelers sometimes takes the form of a serpent. He stops the caravan and, if someone gives him something to eat, indicates the right road to follow. If someone kills this snake the demon does not die: once the body of the reptile has been buried he transforms into an oak tree bearing golden acorns. These acorns will always show the best route to follow if a person keeps two of them in his or her possession.

The household spirit also often takes the form of a serpent. In return for milk he will guarantee the health and prosperity of the cows. If this spirit is killed the cows will stop giving milk. When this spirit is buried it gives birth to a tree that bears golden apples.

The snakes have a king who appears in the form of a reptile with a red beard and a head that shines like gold. He is, in fact, a prince who was transformed into a serpent by a wicked witch. This curse will be lifted from him when his beloved, following the counsel offered by a cat, carries an egg of the *tscharana* on

---

*[This is the theme of gastrostomy: disemboweling is a well-known motif in fairy tales because of its appearance in one of the versions of *Little Red Riding Hood*. —*Trans.*]

her person and becomes pregnant with a *tscharana* who slays the witch.

The English Gypsies say that if you slay the first snake you see you kill your main enemy ("If you more the first sappa you dicks, tute'll more the first enemy you've got").

During Lent is when the "snake of the hazel tree" (*lakora sap*), who has its lair several miles beneath the earth, makes an appearance. It lays its eggs in the roots of the hazel tree. Anyone who can capture or otherwise take possession of one of its eggs will become wealthy.

✦ *King Snake, Tree of All Seeds, Tscharana*

📖 Ficowski, *Le Rameau de l'arbre*, 169–72; Wlislocki, *Volksglaube*, 64, 146; Wlislocki, *Märchen und Sagen*, no. 48; Wlislocki, *Volksdichtungen*, no. 62; *Zanko, chef tribal chez les Chalderash*, 110–14, 127–60; Aichele, *Zigeunermärchen*, no. 18.

SORKOLO: This is one of the sons of Bitoso and the sixth child of Ana, the queen of the *kešalyia*. He takes the form of a tiny, multiheaded worm and causes leg cramps.

✦ *Ana, Bitoso, Kešalyia*

📖 Wlislocki, *Aus dem inneren Leben*, 20.

SOUL (*vodi, dsi*): The Gypsy belief in an external soul kept inside an animal or egg is well attested. If it is the soul of someone who drowned, a chthonic spirit or water spirit (*phuvuš, nivaši*) will hold on to it until the individual's body has completely decomposed. It is only then that this soul can reach the Beyond. But the individual can also come back to life if the spirit releases him or her. An old woman carries away the souls of stillborn children in a sack. A dying animal is able to transfer its soul into the body of a human being. The Gypsies of Transylvania place a bowl of milk next to the exposed corpse so that the soul hovering around its former body can fortify itself before starting its journey to the

Other World. After death the soul also sometimes transforms in to a flower.

✦ *Nivaši, Pçuvuš*

📖 Wlislocki, *Volksdichtungen,* nos. 64, 68, 70; Wlislocki, *Märchen und Sagen,* nos. 13, 25, 35, 55.

SPIDER (*bugaris, gaklin, kakli, spina*): In Gypsy lore the spider was originally a young woman who was forced by a king to make him one item of clothing every day of the week if she wanted her beloved, whom the king had imprisoned, to be released. One day she was too exhausted to even sew a stitch, and the monarch kept her lover in his prison. She perished of despair and was transformed into a spider. When she spins the threads of her webs under the sun and drops of dew can be seen on them, they are her tears.

📖 Leland, *The English Gipsies and Their Language,* 316–17 (*O pū-sūver*).

SQUIRREL (*romaňi mačka,* "Gypsy cat"; *rukheskeri mačka,* "cat of the trees"): The Gypsies view the squirrel as a good luck charm. When one is seen climbing a tree people will rest in its shadow to ensure that journeys and all undertakings are successful. If a squirrel runs alongside a road it is necessary to follow this route to ensure that one will have profitable dealings in the next village. If two lovers come across a squirrel they will live happily and peacefully.

📖 Erzherzog, "Tiere im Glauben der Zigeuner," 51.

STAR (*ćercheň, tscherhenja, tescherbe, širana*): King Sun married a young woman with golden hair, and King Moon wed a girl with silver hair because he could not find one similar to his brother's wife. When both of them had conceived so many children that they no longer had any room for them, they made an agreement that each would devour his own offspring. King Sun respected the pact, but his wife died of grief, and King Moon spared his own children. His brother grew wrathful when he learned of this and has pursued the Moon and his children ever since so that he might eat them. King Sun had let his three most beautiful daughters live, however, and from time to time they travel across the sky tossing meteorites down upon men. Greatly angered by this, Earth, the mother of two boys, forbid her sons from seeing the light of day.

King Moon continued to father children and at times would hurl one to the Earth where it would die immediately and transform into a shell. It should be noted that one of the designations for the stars is *devlerskeri,* "divine light."

According to Zanko, the leader of the Kalderash tribe, the stars are the signs or haloes of mortals. They climb into the sky at birth and fall from it when they die. In Transylvania it is believed that a falling star at the time of a birth heralds a handsome child who will be rich. Jangil Ros' notes that all people have their own star—*lesti Tchalai ando Tcheri*—at birth, and it will die with them. For another etiology of the stars, see the entries for "Sun" and "Man in the Moon."

✦ *King Moon, King Sun*

📖 Wlislocki, *Aus dem inneren Leben,* 67; Wlislocki, *Volksdichtungen,* no. 2; Wlislocki, *Märchen und Sagen,* no. 23; Jangil, *Voyage maison,* 79; Zanko, *chef tribal chez les Chalderash.*

STORK (*cángesli*): It is commonly believed that these birds carry children, and nursing infants are called "storks." Pregnant women pray to the stork for deliverance. Whoever does a good deed for this wading bird will receive gold, precious stones, clothing, and food in the following year.

📖 Wlislocki, *Vom wandernden Zigeunervolke,* 127.

SUN (*kham, kán*): In ancient times there lived an old witch who practiced magic and lived all alone in the sky at night. One day she found a flint in a field and picked it up, and the stone told her that her name was Flint. Then she found a piece of steel, picked him up, and asked it what its name was, and he replied, "Steel." She put them in her pocket and told Flint, "You must marry Master Steel," and she obeyed. But the couple quarreled, and Steel punched his wife in the eye. This made sparks fly and set fire to the witch's pocket. She then threw the burning pocket into the sky and told it to stay there until a man and his wife who never quarreled should come along. The sparks from Flint's eye are the stars, and the fire is the sun.

✦ *King Sun*

📖 Leland, *The Gypsies,* 320–21 (*Sā o kam sos ankerdo*).

SUN AND MOON (*kham and čon*): One day the Sun resolved to get married. For nine years he traveled and searched in vain through the heavens and across the Earth, drawn by his nine horses of fire. So he asked his sister, the beautiful Helen with the silver tresses, if she would marry him, but she refused. The Sun went looking for God, who took him by the hand and brought him to hell to scare him and then to paradise to enchant his soul. After this God asked him to choose between the two. The Sun recklessly chose hell and announced that he would marry Helen there. At the time of the nuptials an invisible hand seized his bride and cast her into the sea, where she became a beautiful silver fish. The Sun grew pale and rose into the sky. Then, as it descended to the west, the Sun dove in to the sea in search of his sister. However, God took the fish in his hand, cast it into the sky, and changed it into the moon. He then condemned the Sun and Moon to pursue each other around the sky for eternity.

✦ *King Moon*

📖 Leland, *The Gypsies,* 345–47.

SUYOLAK: This figure is a hairy giant who is master of the Seven Great Mountains and who knows magic and healing reme-

dies. Witches are referred to as his "wives," and they are compelled
to remove his hairs by licking them, but the hairs always grow
back. During the first time he had intercourse the devils captured
him and chained him to a boulder, where he is still imprisoned
today. If he ever gets free he will destroy the world. On the night
of Pentecost witches gather around his boulder to make him offerings. Suyolak becomes furious at the sight of so many witches and
demons and violently tries to free himself, which causes the rocks
to tremble. Suddenly a large yellow serpent appears and then disappears into the rock, and the prisoner is unable to move a muscle
for almost an entire year.

✦ *Snake, Witch*

📖 Wlislocki, *Aus dem inneren Leben,* 58–59; Wlislocki, "The Worship of
the Mountains," 211–12.

SWALLOW (*devkrlo, schwelma*): Because of the inordinate love they had for their children, a couple quarreled with God incessantly. Finally, weary of their bickering, God ended up cursing them and changed all their children into swallows.

📖 Kabakova and Stroeva, *Contes et Légendes tsiganes*, 127.

TČARIDYI ("the Burning One"): Tčaridyi is the fourth child of Ana, the queen of the *kešalyia*. She is the wife of Tçulo. She has the form of a little hairy worm (*kirmori*). She carries childbed fever (*tçoularidyi*) with which she infects her victims by leaving several of her hairs on their bodies. Pregnant women should abstain from eating crayfish, otherwise they will attract Tčaridyi or one of her children. On the day of the feast of the Immaculate Conception women make offerings to Tçulo and to Tčaridyi consisting of omelets with squash seeds. Once each person present has taken a bite, a sorceress will deposit them in the hole of a hollow tree and recite a prayer asking Ana to keep Tçulo and Tčaridyi away and to spare the bodies of the women present.

✦ *Ana, Kešalyia, Tçulo*

📖 Wlislocki, *Aus dem inneren Leben*, 12–15.

TÇULO ("the Fat One"): He is the third child of Ana, the queen of the *kešalyia*. He is described as looking like a ball covered with prickers.

When he rolls around inside someone's body he causes pains in the lower abdomen. After eating a crayfish and a beetle on the advice of his son Melálo, the king of the *loçolicos* slept with his wife, Ana, which resulted in her giving birth to Tçulo.

Tçulo and Tçaridyi

Since then he continually tries to prevent women from procreating and is responsible for those who die during labor. When this happens the Gypsies of Transylvania say, "Tçulo was mad at his wife."

✦ *Ana, Loçolicos, Kešalyia, Melálo, Tçaridyi*

📖 Wlislocki, *Aus dem inneren Leben,* 10–12.

THREAD OF THE VIRGIN: To avoid being infertile Gypsy women gather the threads of the Virgin spun by the *meta segmentata*. They then eat them with their husbands while reciting a charm that invokes the *kešalyia* and invites them to attend the baptism of their future baby.

✦ *Kešalyia*

📖 Wlislocki, *Vom wandernden Zigeunervolke,* 88.

THREE MARYS (THE): ✦ Gospels of the Gypsies

THUNDER STONE: This stone, the ceraunia, is often confused for the glossopetrae (which is also known as a "tongue stone").

📖 Wlislocki, "The Worship of the Mountains," 215; Wislocki, *Aus dem inneren Leben,* 63–75; Berger, "Mythologie der Zigeuner," 811–12; Lecouteux, *A Lapidary of Sacred Stones,* 95–96 (ceraunia, caranitis).

THUNDERSTORM (hrimšagos, timle vetra, devleskero, tschiro): The storm erupted when the devil (*Beng*) defied God (*Pouro Del*) and tried to seize power. The thunder is the voice of God in his wrath.

✦ *Devil*

📖 Jangil, *Voyage maison*, 77.

TOAD (*grapodo*): This animal can sometimes be the provider of wealth. As a sign of his gratitude toward an old woman who gave him welcome, a toad laid golden ducats for her every night. When this woman died nothing was found but her clothing, as she had left, young and beautiful again, with the enchanted toad. As for the ducats she had left behind in a chest, they transformed in to stones—to the great dismay of her heirs!

📖 Ficowski, *Le Rameau de l'arbre*, 215–19.

TREASURE: The dream of wealth constantly recurs in numerous folktales and legends. In one story an individual must dig by hand at the foot of a tree and keep his eyes closed until he hears a shout ring out. Of course the person feels a compelling urge to open his eyes, but he resists this temptation and finds a treasure.

One can also find a treasure with the help of a magic wand that is held in a specific way (with the little fingers turned toward each other and the thumbs pointing toward the sky). This causes the treasure to emit a flame that appears above the ground, at which point the person should walk around the spot three times while reciting a conjuration to the *pçuvuš*.

> Pçuvuš man, pçuvuš man!
> If I can find the gold
> I will rescue you!
> I will make three chains,
> One for God, so good and kind

I will make from pure gold;
For Jesus Christ, the child of God,
I will use shining silver;
The third chain, I will have made
For Mary, the most beautiful of women!
In the name of God, go away from me!

It is believed that wasps are the guardians of buried treasure.

✦ *Pçuvuš, Wasp*

📖 Ficowski, *Le Rameau de l'arbre*, 185; Wlislocki, *Vom wandernden Zigeunervolke*, 152–53; Wlislocki, *Volksdichtungen*, 96.

TREE (*ploko, ruk*): Thousands and thousands of years ago trees knew how to walk. A miser forced an oak tree to follow his commands. He ordered it to carry him, to kill a bull so that he might have some meat, and then to pick up a cask of wine. Having no stove on which to grill his meat, the miser, passing in front of a church, demanded that the oak take the bell. When the oak complied with his orders lightning struck him as well as the miser, the bull, and the cask. Since that time trees have rooted themselves into the ground and no longer walk.

📖 Wlislocki, *Volksdichtungen*, 191–93.

TREE OF ALL SEEDS (*save sumbreskro kašt*): This is a cosmic tree that stands atop the highest mountain on Earth—created when King Sun lifted the dress of his mother, the Earth (*Pçuv*)—whose summit penetrates into the "highest heaven" (*baro cero*). It is also a tree of life, the mere sight of which will cause the rejuvenation of the person who sees it. It blossoms in the sky and carries all the seeds of the Earth. Nine black dogs defend it in every direction, and a gigantic serpent is biting its roots, which is reminiscent of a representation of Scandinavian mythology: the serpent Nidhögg gnawing upon the roots of the cosmic tree Yggdrasill. The Tree of All Seeds corresponds to the Gaokerena of Iranian myths from which flows the elixir of immortality (Avestan *haoma,* equivalent to the Vedic Sanskrit *soma*). The Zoroastrian *Bundahishn* (*The First Creation*), chapter 18 reads: "The tree of all seeds sprouted up in the middle of the Vourukasha Sea; it carries the seeds of all plants."

Lightning bolts flash at the top of this tree and steal its leaves, which they bring to the spirits of the waters, the *nivàshà.* These spirits then give them to the women with whom they spend time and teach them how to use them, thereby training them to be sorceresses (*covalyi*). The leaves will retain their virtues for a period of nine years.

By performing the "marriage" of a fir tree and a willow—that is to say, when they are planted next to one another and a red thread is tied around them—a person who leans over the ground can see the Tree of All Seeds on Christmas night.

✦ *King Sun, Marriage of the Trees, Nivaši*

📖 Wlislocki, *Vom wandernden Zigeunervolke,* 146–47; Wlislocki, "The Worship of the Mountains," 165–66; Wlislocki, *Volksglaube,* 137–41; Wlislocki, *Volksdichtungen,* 222–23.

TSCHALE, TÇALE: This is the name of a Gypsy tribe in Transylvania. The word is derived from *tçalo,* "full, satisfied." A handsome lad ate with an appetite of twenty men without ever being sated, which is what earned him this name. He was hired to be a servant of the king, who gave him the task to leave his home and not return there during the day or during the night, nor with bare feet or wearing shoes, and once he has returned to stay neither inside nor out. After he successfully passed this test the young man married and fathered many children, all of whom were as insatiable as he himself. The king eventually drove them out of his kingdom. The Tçale are the descendants of this family; they have hearty appetites but very little to eat.

📖 Wlislocki, *Vom wandernden Zigeunervolke,* 73–74.

TSCHARANA: ✦ Čarana

TSYGANKA (fem. *Tsigane*): According to a Russian legend this is the name of the wife of Pharaoh, worshipper of the Golden Calf. He wanted his wife to share his worship, but she was Jewish. Because she refused to concede to his wishes he locked her in a dungeon equipped with nine locks. It was she who advised Moses to flee Egypt. Once she arrived in Bessarabia she had a son who married a Moldavian. Their children are the ancestors of the Gypsies.

✦ *Pharavono*

📖 *Journal of the Gypsy Lore Society,* 3rd series, vol. 17 (1939), 130–32; Berger, "Mythologie der Zigeuner," 791.

TUBALCAIN: ✦ Pantheon

URME, URMA, URMÁ (pl. *Urma*): The Urma are spirits who appear in the form of very tall women (*baro trupos*) who possess a singular beauty. They are always dressed in white and thus are also known as "White Ladies" (*parne romni, parne gadsiori*). In the lore of the Gypsies of southern Hungary they have wings and can fly.

They are the fairies of fate, and even guardian angels, as is made glaringly apparent when one of these Urma tells a young man, "I am a good fairy (*láce Urme*) who at the moment you were born, swore a promise to protect and to help you." They live in sparkling palaces that stand on the mountains created by King Sun and are called the Blessed Mountains (*baçtolo bar*), where they frolic and dance on moonlit nights. The eldest of these fairies is called Lace Urme, "the good fairy," and is the guardian spirit. The younger spirit is called Šilale Urme, "the cold fairy"; she bears this name because her wishes and prophecies are halfway between those of her oldest and her youngest sisters. The latter sister is called Miseçe Urme, "the wicked fairy," who brings nothing but maladies and suffering to men. She looks like a horrible old crone, or she assumes the form of a frog. She lives in a castle that is surrounded by a wasteland or a river of fire, details that situate her dwelling between this world and the Other World. In front of her door stands a fountain of burning water. This wicked fairy owns a magic mirror that will turn anyone who gazes into it to stone. She has a dragon son whose perspiration is blood and whose hairs, once they have been burned and ingested, allow a person to go instantaneously wherever he or she desires. She can rejuvenate, provided her body is cut up into pieces and cooked in a cauldron. Wicked fairies possess a cloak that renders the wearer invisible. In one story one of them owns a cow with golden horns.

There is a curious tale that recounts how a woman who was disconsolate because she could not have a child saw an Urme appear who bade her to suckle on its breasts. She obeyed the fairy and later gave birth to twins. But the Urme also had her breasts sucked by a dog and a mare, who gave birth to twins intended to be two boys. She then dug two holes in the ground, poured some of her breast milk into them, and two oak trees grew out of them. This story illustrates the belief in an animal and plant double (alter ego) for every individual.

On the night following an infant's birth the Urma will appear and set its destiny. To attract Urma blessings, people perform certain magical practices during the three nights after the birth. A furrow is dug around the mother and child, inside of which datura seeds are placed. This will drive away any evil spirits who wish ill to the Urma. A bowl with a blend of honey is also set out for these fairies. Each Urme can only bestow her favor on seven people. If she transgresses this prohibition she is doomed to perish miserably. One of these fairies punished an evil king—who, when he was bored and sought to amuse himself, had several people sawed in half right before his eyes—by spitting on the ground. This caused mice to come out who devoured the evil monarch.

The good Urma have good children; the wicked ones give birth to half-Urma who live like quarrelsome mortals. They will marry humans on the condition that their husbands respect one prohibition, such as not to try to find out what their wives are doing at night, which is nursing the Čarana. When Urma have children from a mortal father they give birth to three at a time. The Urma will nurse these children just once, and they are already able to walk. They soon leave their mother and go live in hollow trees. Once they have grown into adulthood they have permission to enter the palace of their queen, Matuyá.

The good Urma are not able to overcome the wicked Urma who sometimes assume the form of frogs (sambá). It is believed that the Urma look kindly on livestock. The Polish Gypsies regard these fairies as guardian spirits.

The Gypsies believe that if a cow urinates while it is being milked this is a sure sign that the animal has been bewitched. When this happens some of the cow's urine is collected and mixed with onion peels and the egg from a black hen. This mixture is then boiled. It is then added to the animal's food while saying:

> *Ko ándré hin, avriává!*
> *Trin Urma cingárden les,*
> *Trin Urma tráden les,*
> *Andre yándengré ker*
> *Beshél yov ándre ker.*
> *Hin leske máy yakhá,*
> *Hin leske máy páña!*

> Make come out what is inside!
> Three Urma call it,
> Three Urma bring it,
> In the shell of an egg
> It lives in this house.
> It has plenty of fire,
> It has plenty of water!

Then half the egg is thrown into running water while the other half is tossed into a fire.

✦ *Blessed Mountains, Čarana, Datura, Egg, Frog, Matuyá*

📖 Wlislocki, *Aus dem inneren Leben*, 2, 56; Wlislocki, *Volksglaube*, 2–11, 41; Wlislocki, *Märchen und Sagen*, no. 52; Wlislocki, *Volksdichtungen*, nos. 35–36, 38, 47, 54; Wlislocki, "Urmen: Schicksalsfrauen der Zigeuner," 133–36; Berger, "Mythologie der Zigeuner," 816–17; Tillhagen, *Zigeunermärchen und -geschichten*, 115–21; Leland, *Gypsy Sorcery and Fortune Telling*, 86, 90–91.

URSITORY (*Ursitori, Ursitele, Urditele, Osatorele, Ursoi, Ursoni*): These are wondrously beautiful women who allot human beings with their fates. Despite many similarities they are not another form of the Urma, with whom they are often confused. They live in the mountains where they have splendid underground palaces, and they are fond of singing and dancing under the trees. When they unite with a mortal man they give birth to three daughters all at once and then immediately grow old. They only nurse their children once. These children, like those of the Urma, can run on the day of their birth, so they also leave their mother at once to live inside hollow trees. Once they are adults they

have the right to move in to the palace of their queen, Matuyá.

One of the three sisters—in contrast to the other two—is always ill-intentioned toward human beings.

✦ *Armiko, Matuyá, Urme*

📖 Berger, "Mythologie der Zigeuner," 815–16; Wlislocki, *Volksglaube,* 41; Maximoff, *Les Ursitory;* Brednich, "Les sources folkloriques du roman tsigane: *les Ursitory* de Matéo Maximoff."

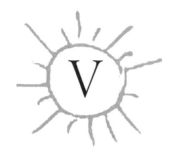

VAMPIRE: ✦ Čohano, Múlo

VIOLIN (hegedúva, mangri, bošc, šetra, bašipangre, gajga):
A young man, imprisoned for having sought to marry a princess, received a visit in his dungeon cell from the fairy Matuyá, who gave him a box and a stick and urged him to take several hairs from her head and attach them to these two objects. She then told him to touch the hairs that had been stretched over the box—into which the fairy had laughed and cried—with the stick. The music that came out of this instrument when the young man played it had the power to fill the heart with joy or sorrow. Thanks to this instrument the young man was able to wed the princess.

According to another etiology the violin owes its origin to the devil. In return for helping Mara, a young maiden in love with a huntsman who was indifferent to her charms, the devil demanded that she let him have her four brothers. He changed them in to four strings. After this he demanded to also have her father, whom he transformed in to the sound box, and her mother, whom he made in to a bow, and he demanded a long hair from the manes of Mara's horses. Then Mara played the instrument and won the heart of her beloved (*pireno*), but the

devil carried off both of them. Some time later a Gypsy came along and picked up the violin, which had been left lying on the ground of the forest.

In a riddle the violin is presented this way:

> Four strings, on the wood,
> A stick garnished with horsehair
> Will invite to dance
> The entire company.

There is also a Gypsy proverb that says: "A violin without strings is like a house without a wife."

The Serbian Gypsies believe that God created the violin in the back of Saint Peter, who made him fall when he was entering a tavern. He asked God the reason for this and was told that he had created the instrument so that Gypsies could entertain people and make them happy.

✦ *Matuyá*

📖 Wlislocki, *Vom wandernden Zigeunervolke,* 221–23; Groome, *Gypsy Folk-Tales,* no. 37; Ficowski, *Le Rameau de l'arbre,* 158; Kabakova and Stroeva, *Contes et légendes tziganes,* 158.

VOSESKO MANUŠ: ✦ Man of the Woods

VYUSHENGRI, RUVANUSH ("wolf-man"): The name of this werewolf is formed from *ruv,* "wolf," and *manush/manuš,* "man." The metamorphosis is caused by an evil spell that a witch has cast, or because a witch has sucked out a victim's blood from a distance. Sometimes changed into dogs, these men accompany the witches in their nocturnal descents. Nomadic Gypsies clip the tail off every dog that falls into their hands, which will prevent it from changing back in to a man if it is one that had been earlier transformed by a witch.

It is difficult to tell the *ruvanuš* from the Čohano.

✦ *Čohano*

📖 Wlislocki, "The Witch of the Gypsies," 40–41.

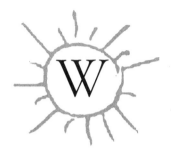

WASP (*birilyi, perreli*): Just like the bumblebee, the wasp is considered to be a companion of the chthonic spirits (*phuvuš*) and the guardian of their treasure.

✦ *Pçuvuš*

📖 Wlislocki, *Vom wandernden Zigeunervolke,* 130.

WATER LILY: This concerns the tale of a young woman transformed in to a white water lily by her stepmother, a sorceress who owned a magic ball of yarn, because the girl wished to flee with her beloved. In exchange for eggs and apples three *nivashi* kissed the water lily and restored her to her original form; they then lured the sorceress to the river, where they drowned her.

📖 Wlislocki, *Volksdichtungen,* no. 24.

WATER NYMPH: A Russian folktale relates the story of two sisters who are transformed by the sorcerer of the caverns because they refuse their destiny. One is transformed in to a *rusalka* (*лесная русалка/ речная русалка*), a "water nymph," of the woods and the other into a *rusalka* of the river. The third sister, who accepts her fate, is adopted by the King of the Sea.

During the winter they live at the bottom of the rivers. On Trinity Sunday they leave the waters to inhabit the woods and fields, choosing a birch or weeping willow in which to stay.

It is clear that the term "water nymph" is actually referring to a different kind of mythic reality here, since these beings inhabit both the forests and the rivers. The three sisters are supernatural spirits punished for having transgressed against the order of the all-powerful destiny, most likely embodied by a god. The Slavic figure of the *rusalka* was adopted into the Gypsy folklore of Eastern Europe.

📖 Druts and Gessler, *Skazki i pesni tsgan Rossii*, 116–19; Gruel-Apert, *Le Monde mythologique russe*, 67–75.

WEASEL (*phurdini*, "the one who huffs and puffs"; *lisla*): If you rub the body of a dead person with a weasel skin, while the fiancé is holding the deceased's hand, the person can be brought back to life, but their hand will remain stuck to that of their beloved. The belief that the skin of a weasel can revive the dead has existed since Classical Antiquity. Marie de France echoes this belief in her medieval lai *Eliduc* (verse 1032ff.). The skin of the weasel that the Bohemians use for magical purposes reputedly draws its power from the *chagrin* (*chagrino, ḥágrin*).

If, when encountering a person, a weasel arches up and starts snorting, this is a dreadful sign. In the case of a pregnant woman it means the birth will be difficult. If a weasel crosses the paths of nomads it is a sign that they must change direction, and they leave a signal at this spot—which is generally a stick stuck into the ground to which some hairs have been attached—for other members of the tribe.

✦ *Chagrin*

📖 Ficowski, *Le Rameau de l'arbre*, 176–77; Erzherzog, "Tiere im Glauben der Zigeuner," 50.

WHISKER: ✦ Hair

WHITE DOE: This animal plays a role in a curious legend about soul transfer. The doe killed a young woman who tried to stop her from eating the hay that had been stored by the tribe and then kissed her and breathed her own soul into the girl's body. From that time on the young woman would go out every night to steal hay. Her fiancé captured her, covered her with snow, and then his mother brought her back to life with her human soul.

📖 Ficowski, *Le Rameau de l'arbre*, 173–77; Wlislocki, *Märchen und Sagen*, no. 5.

WHITE DOG (*párno ĵuko/ ĵukel, dschukklo***):** Every Gypsy tribe owns a white dog. By licking the soles of its feet, it helps people on their deathbeds to cross over by luring their souls out of their bodies. This psychopomp function brings to mind, as Wlislocki points out, the Parsi belief that a dying individual will not die in peace if his or her eyes are not resting on a dog who has been reserved for just this purpose. White dogs are also the guardians of the Other World, which is located in the mountains of King Wind.

In Gypsy legends the white dog is also a man who regains his original form once a year if a young woman kisses him. This woman gave birth to a white puppy and committed suicide, but when her body was fished out of the water the puppy began to suckle on her, and this restored her to life.

To cure the bite of a rabid dog a prayer is addressed to a white dog of the Other World (*parne jiukleya ande them mulengre*) that asks him to carry away the "poison" to the home of the dead so that they might burn it.

✦ *Other World, King Wind*

📖 Wlislocki, *Aus dem inneren Leben*, 280; Wlislocki, "The Worship of the Mountains," 213; Wlislocki, *Volksdichtungen*, 327–29; Wlislocki, *Märchen und Sagen*, 33–37; Wlislocki, *Volksglaube*, 162; Wlislocki, "Gebräuche der transsilvanischen Zigeuner," 23.

WILD HUNT: ✦ Efta Shellengeri

WILL-O'-THE-WISP: Some English Gypsies call will o' the wisps "light ghosts" (*avali*) and others call them "little ghosts" (*Momeli*) or use the English term. They lead travelers astray and seek to lure them into the water and then turn around and roar at them with laughter. Will-o'-the-wisps have been conflated with goblins that are two feet tall.

   📖 Leland, *The English Gipsies and Their Language,* Gudlo XXXIV.

WITCH (*holyipi*): Witches are called the "wives of Suyolak," a hairy giant to whom they give offerings on the night of Pentecost. They can transform men in to horses by tossing a bridle around their necks, and they can also turn them in to dogs. Witches hold their sabbath on a Friday night, when they renew their pact with the devil, which entails making him drink the menstrual blood that they have set aside for seven years for just this purpose.

   ✦ *Mountains of the Moon, Ruvanush, Suyolak, Vyushengri, Water Lily*

WOLFMAN: ✦ Vyushengri, Ruvanush

WORM (sg. *kirmo*, pl. *kirmora*): For the Gypsies, worms are the form taken by the forces to which the Gypsies attribute external pains and ailments. Similar beliefs can be found among many other peoples.

   To treat such cases they go out before dawn to harvest the spurge plant (*euphorbia*), which is known as *rukeskro tçud,* "wolf's milk." They mix it with garlic, salt, and water, boiling these ingredients together to make a broth. They smear it on the afflicted area and throw whatever is left over into the river while reciting the following charm.

> *Kirmora jánen ándre tçud,*
> *Andrál tçud, andré sir,*
> *Andrál sir, andré páñi,*

Panensá kiyá dádeske,
Kiyá Niváseske,
Pçandel tumen shelchá
Eñávárdesh teñá!

Worms go into the milk,
From the milk into the garlic,
From the garlic into the water,
With the water to (your) father,
To the Niváši,
He shall bind you with a rope
Ninety-nine (yards long)!

When the spirit or life (*jipen*) of a witch, which is to say her double, transforms into a worm, it devours the heart of the person whom it has entered. It will suck away at the heart bit by bit, causing the person to go in to a gradual decline. One way to protect yourself from this form of attack is to rub your torso with garlic before going to bed.

  📖 Leland, *Gypsy Sorcery and Fortune Telling*, 95; Wlislocki, *Volksglaube*, 118–19.

WORM OF GOOD FORTUNE (*kirmo báçtálo*):

Whoever finds an egg of the "mother owl" (*ratyakri day*), the thousand-year-old owl, on Easter beneath a hazel tree can easily gain possession of this kind of worm. This is the time when the owl lays and buries her eggs beneath a hazel tree (*o akhor*), and, seven years later, these eggs will contain a worm who can make its owner a very wealthy and happy person.

  📖 Wlislocki, *Vom wandernden Zigeunervolke*, 153; Wlislocki, *Volksdichtungen*, no. 50.

YADO: The terrestrial chasm that welcomes the evil men who turn in to *múlo* and return by night to torment humans. Yado corresponds to the Christian hell.

✦ *Múlo*

📖 Jangil, *Voyage maison*, 79.

YAGSHI: The name for the demons of fire and lightning.

✦ *Pantheon*

YEHWAH, YAHWAH (Eve): This name is enigmatic because it is written like that of God: YHVH (Yahweh). The Spanish Gypsies call Eve "Hayan," a Hebrew name that derives from the verb *hayah,* meaning "to be, to live." In both Gypsy and Jewish beliefs the first wife of Adam was Lilith, who came before Eve.

✦ *Anthropogeny*

YEVENDIKRA: The nomadic Gypsies who live in the regions around the Danube, Serbia, and southern Hungary divide winter into three periods. There is "little winter" (*cigno yevend*), which spans the period from the first snow to Saint Andrew's Day; the "great winter" (*baro yevend*), which runs from that date until the middle of February; and then the "little winter" returns. This period extends from mid-February until the ice has disappeared entirely. At the beginning of the first winter the women cook as many cakes as there are members of the family, and then the head of the household kills a rooster (*báshno*) and his wife kills a hen. Before dawn the two roasted chickens and the cakes are placed outside, and the inhabitants of the caves gather in front of their homes. The eldest among them recites a prayer asking God to protect the entire family from sickness, sorrow, and want during the forthcoming winter. Then everyone present bows to the east and heads to the table. The men eat the hens and the women eat the roosters. Then the youngest woman who is present gathers the bones and casts them into the fire while saying a prayer that asks God to provide harmony for each couple.

📖 Wlislocki, *Volksglaube,* 135.

TEXTS

I. THE GREAT FLOOD

Once upon a time, humans lived forever. They experienced no worries and were not tormented by any pains, cold, or disease. The earth produced the finest fruits, meat grew on trees, and many of the rivers flowing through the land contained milk or wine instead of water. Men and animals lived in harmony with each other, and no one had the slightest fear of death.

But one day it happened that an old man came into their land and asked a man if he could give him shelter for the night. He slept in the humble cottage and was treated with fine hospitality by the man's wife. When he resumed his journey the next morning the old man gave his host a small fish in a bowl and told him, "Guard it well and do not eat it! When I return in nine days, if you return it to me, I will richly reward you." Then he left.

The lady of the house looked at the fish and asked her husband, "What do you think about roasting this fish, dear husband?"

"I promised the old man that I would take good care of it and give it back to him," he responded. "Swear to me that you will leave it alone and keep it safe until he comes back!" She promised she would, saying, "I shall not kill it, and I will keep it safe, if God so wills."

Two days went by, and the woman said to herself, "I wonder what this fish would taste like? It must be delicious since that old man prizes it so, not wanting to cook it and bringing it with him everywhere he goes." She turned this thought over and over again in her mind, eventually taking the fish out of its bowl and placing it on a grill. But at that exact moment, just as she committed her misdeed, the very first bolt of lightning to ever strike the Earth came down and killed her. She was the very first person to ever be killed on Earth.

Then it began raining heavily, and the rivers overflowed their banks and flooded the entire countryside. On the ninth day the old man reappeared and told his host, "You swore an oath to not kill that fish. Choose yourself another wife, gather your entire family together, and build a boat that will allow you to save yourself and your family. All of humanity and all of the animals are going to be drowned; you alone shall be spared. So you must also take animals and the seeds of all the trees and plants so that you can repopulate the world later. The old man then disappeared, and the man did all that he had been commanded to do.

It rained for an entire year, and nothing could be seen at all except for the water and the sky. After the year had passed the water began to recede, and the man disembarked, accompanied by his second wife and all their relatives, as well as all the animals. They then found themselves in the position of having to work, build, and sow crops to survive. Pain and exhaustion were their daily lot. Added to the suffering of their labor were the evils of illness and death, which made it so that they were very slow to multiply, and thousands of years had to run their course before they again became as numerous as they once were, and as they still are today.

📖 Wlislocki, *Vom wandernden Zigeunervolke*, 267–69.

II. THE WHITE HIND

During a very severe winter the people of the Ashani tribe were settled by the edge of a large forest. Everyone was shivering and trembling at the prospect of even colder days and nights to come. One evening when they were all gathered in the tent of their chieftain to discuss how to protect themselves from the ferocity of the winter, Rika, the pretty daughter of their leader, challenged them: "Do you really think you can get us out of this situation by arguing among yourselves? You need to give more thought to the way we might kill the white hind who comes every night to eat our hay reserves!" This was a very serious problem. When the men tried to get near this animal it would retreat into the depths of the forest and disappear. Bullets could not hurt it; they just bounced off its chest. Traps and snares were useless against her. Even the most audacious and courageous members of the tribe had given up their pursuit of this invulnerable white hind and simply let it eat all their meager reserves of hay.

Silence greeted Rika's words, and the men soon returned to their personal living quarters. The next day the entire camp was abuzz with a huge piece of news: Rika had slain the white hind. Sometime during the night before she had managed to kill the invincible animal with several blows of an ax. The story had already circulated a hundred times through the camp when the Bohemians all returned to the chieftain's tent that evening to discuss the major event of the day one more time. They had not yet seen their leader at all that day. When they got there they found Rika, the flower of the tribe, standing apart from the men and hiding her stricken face in her hands. She sadly greeted the arrivals, and when one of the men began speaking about the white hind, she cried out, "I did not kill it! I lied, I did not do anything!"

"What are you saying, Rika?" the others asked in surprise.

"I did not kill the white hind," she repeated.

Everyone burst out lauging, and one of them said, "We saw its corpse with our own eyes—it was lying in the forest, and with our own eyes we saw you kill it. We were scared and had little desire to come to your aid. So tell us how you did it and what happened after that."

"Okay," the cheiftain's daughter replied. "I went outside during the night, and I saw the white hind devouring our hay reserves. I quickly grabbed an ax. I hid behind a stack of hay, and, when the beast approached, I cast the ax against its forehead, but it bounced off and fell to the ground. The hind rushed upon me and knocked me upside down. All my bones broke, and I was dead. I only remember that the white hind leaned over me, kissed my mouth, and blew her soul into my body. Alas, I am a hind! Alas, I must leave!"

She suddenly rushed outside and vanished into the forest.

Stunned, the Bohemians consoled their leader, who was weeping in a corner. Everyone was grieving, but nobody's suffering was equal to that of Dimo, who was in love with Rika. With a heavy heart he slipped back to his tent and told his old blind mother what had just happened. "That is a terrible story," she said. "From now on Rika will emerge from the forest every night to eat our hay. You must try to slay her before the night of the star Čaraya. I will see then what I might be able to do."

This is what happened next. During the day Rika wandered around the forest in sorrow, but in the evening she would come out only to return to its depths exhausted at dawn the next day. The first lark had returned from its journey to the land of eternal summer, and the night of the star Čaraya had arrived. Dimo, Rika's lover, went out that night and waited with his ax for his sweetheart to come near the haystacks. He suddenly spotted two sandals she was in the habit of wearing, then a red shawl flying over them. The moonlight grew stronger, and Dimo realized that the shawl and the sandals were moving, and he heard a soft rustling in the hay as if the wind was gently blowing through the stack. He grabbed his ax and brought it down forcefully onto the red shawl. A cry rang out, and then there was the chieftain's daughter, Rika, lying dead at the feet of her beloved. Dimo hoisted her body onto his shoulders and carried it to his blind mother. He sat down, tightly embracing the young woman in his arms. Meanwhile, the old woman took out the skin of a weasel, opened the belly of the dead woman, and slid this skin into the incision she had made along with a red substance, which she alone knew the secret of how to prepare. The young woman came back to life, and Dimo was ecstatic when he saw his fiancée had been resurrected. But when she tried to stand up it proved to be impossible, because she had been welded to Dimo's body. "Woe is us!" said the old woman. "God is punishing you for loving each other too greatly." Dimo and Rika fled into the forest at some point during the night and have never been seen since.

III. THE MOUNTAIN OF CATS

There was a poor widow with only one son, who fed her thanks to his work and who would share with her even the smallest slice of bread. She was already old and fragile, and if she had not had this kind son to look after her she would have been hard pressed to make do during her declining years. But she was able to live without concerns, for she knew her son would provide for all her needs. Now one evening, when her son was beginning to head back home from the fields, he encountered a *phuvuš*. He had heard that whoever could pull out a hair from a *phuvuš* without it noticing would become rich. In fact, every stone he touched with this hair would turn in to gold. He let the *phuvuš* pass by, and he pretended as if he had not seen it. Then he swiftly turned around, followed it discretely, and suddenly swooped in to try to steal one of its hairs without its knowledge. But the *phuvuš* caught sight of him, turned around, and slammed the lad to the ground. He then picked him up, threw him over his shoulders, and disappeared. Several people had witnessed this scene from a distance, and on their way home they stopped in at the widow's house to tell her what they had seen. Beside herself with grief, the poor woman wept day and night. Finally the day came that she ran out of all her provisions, and she now had to find work to earn her daily bread. From that day on she would go out into the forest to gather berries and sticks that she would sell in the village.

One day she got lost in the forest. She continued to wander farther into its depths and ended up finding herself on the Mountain of Cats. This is where hundreds of souls of the dead lived who had been transformed into cats.* Several black cats came running up to her on the poor woman's arrival and demanded to know: "What are you looking for here?" She told them her story. After they heard it the cats told her, "Be our servant for three weeks; when the new moon appears in the sky we will let you leave, and you will have no cause to regret the time that you have spent with us." The old woman thought to herself, "What can I do all alone at the house? I may just as well stay here!" And she said, "Yes, I will stay with you!" The cats then indicated to her the work, which she could perform with ease. In exchange they gave her succulent dishes and delicious wines. She was beginning to give thought to spending the rest of her life with these cats when the three weeks were up and the new moon appeared in the night sky. The oldest cat of the mountain then came to speak to her. "You have served us faithfully and honestly for three weeks," he told her. "Take this stone in payment, go back to the spot where the *phuvuš* took

---

*In the folklore of the Bohemian Gypsies the souls of the dead who sinned greatly during their lives are often transformed in to black cats and must spend a good many years in this form before they are redeemed and can make their way to the kingdom of the dead.

your son, touch the ground with the stone, and your child will be freed immediately and be able to return home with you."* The cat then handed a glittering stone to the old woman and led her back through the forest to the area from where she would be able to easily find her way back home. But instead of proceeding directly home the widow instead sought out the place where her son had vanished with the *phuvuš*. She touched the ground with the stone as the cat had instructed, the earth opened immediately, and her son came out. Both the poor mother and her good son shared a moment of joy. Once they returned back home they lived from that day forth in good luck and prosperity, because every piece of iron that they touched with the glittering stone on the night of the new moon would immediately turn in to pure gold.

📖 Wlislocki, *Volksdichtungen*, no. 42.

IV. THE BRIDE OF THE *PHUVUŠ*

Once upon a time there was a poor man who had only one child, a girl who was wondrously beautiful. He was destitute and could barely get by from day to day, but even when he could not find work in the village they still could make ends meet because folk gladly found some task for the beautiful young girl to do so that she could earn some money. Never did the poor man go to bed with an empty belly. Every day his daughter gave him good dishes and brandy, whether or not he had been able to earn a little money. However, he was perpetually sad, and no one had ever seen him smile since the day his wife was buried. The local people wrongly imagined that he was still mourning his wife, but he was

*According to Gypsy folklore, when the new moon is in the night sky the black cats deposit a glittering stone that only remains on the surface of the ground for the length the time it takes to count to seven. It then vanishes into the earth. With this stone a person can open anything that has been sealed and transform all metals in to gold.

afflicted by something entirely different. On the death of his wife almost seven years earlier he did not have even a single kreutzer in his pocket for buying a coffin and paying the priest. Once his wife had closed her eyes for the last time he went out to the field where he sat upon a boundary marker and wept bitterly. A *phuvuš* popped out of a hole just then and said to him, "Two men who were passing by here said that you could not afford to have your wife buried! I will help you and give you the money you need for the coffin and to pay the priest if you promise to give me your daughter when seven years are up. I want her to be my wife!" The man thought on this for a while and finally replied, "Fine, I will give you my daughter in seven years." The *phuvuš* gave him several pieces of gold, and the man was able to have his wife's funeral. But sorrow had been his constant companion since that day, and no one had ever seen him laugh.

The seven years soon sped by. The child became a beautiful young woman, and a handsome lad named Anrus (Andreas) loved her. He wished to marry her at the next Carnaval. Their marriage day was drawing near when one night the father said to his daughter, "Come with me to the field!" She followed her father, and, when they entered the place where the *phuvuš* had given him the gold pieces some seven years earlier, the father ordered his daughter: "Stay here my child, I am going to go gather some wood in the forest." He kissed her and returned to the village as quick as his feet could carry him. The *phuvuš* emerged from his hole and carried the beautiful young girl underground, to where his own country was located.

The next evening Anrus came by to ask about his beloved. The poor man told him that his daughter had been abducted by a *phuvuš* the night before. Inconsolable, Anrus had the father take him to the spot where his beloved had disappeared. When the man showed him the hole the young man immediately climbed down into it but was forced to turn back before he had gone too far, because a large stone barred the entrance into the land of the *phuvuša*. When he came back to the surface Anrus told the unhappy father, "Go back home! I am going to stay there until I find some way to get in."

While the poor father remained sitting all alone in his cabin, Anrus waited for the *phuvuš* in front of his lair in the field. Eventually the creature appeared. When he saw Anrus he asked him, "What do you want here?"

"I am looking for work and am unable to find anything," the lad responded.

"Follow me to the country of the *phuvuša*. I am personally going to find you a job!"

Anrus agreed to this and followed him. When they reached the large stone the *phuvuš* pulled a red egg from his pocket. He touched the boulder with it, and it immediately moved to the side and they entered the dark land of the *phuvuša*. He put the red egg back in his pocket and took out a white egg that rolled before them giving off a light that was as bright as the sun. They passed before many small houses in which numerous *phuvuša* were living. Once they had reached the home of his guide, Anrus caught sight of his bride sitting in the corner weeping and gestured to her not to utter a word. The *phuvuš* then told the young man, "This young lady is going to be my wife after tomorrow, and you must, just as if it were me, obey and do whatever she commands you to do. Here is a black hen. You must give it food and water every day, but you are forbidden to ever touch it, for then it will die and I will be forced to kill you." Anrus promised to do everything he was asked and therefore became the servant of the *phuvuš*. He took care of the hen, swept the house, and kept busy all day long.

The next day the *phuvuš* went back up to the surface, and Anrus was able to speak with his bride. "How are we going to be able to get back home?" she asked him.

"I don't know. But I would rather see you dead than see you become the wife of that horrible *phuvuš*."

"Do you know why you must keep watch over that black hen the way you do?" she responded. "I am going to tell you! That idiot explained to me that there are three eggs in this hen: one red, one white, and one black. The black contains his strength; nothing can happen to the person who has it in his possession, and if it is thrown into the water, this will kill the *phuvuš.*"

Overjoyed, Anrus replied, "Tonight, when he is sleeping, I will touch the hen and it will die. We will take the eggs and make our way back to the surface!" And so they did.

That evening the *phuvuš* returned and went to bed. As the *phuvuš* slept, Anrus touched the black hen, which killed it. He took the three eggs out of its stomach and stuffed them into his bag. Then he left with his bride. Once they stepped out of the little house they could not see a thing, but Anrus pulled the white egg from his bag and placed it on the ground. It rolled slowly before them, emitting a light that was as bright as the sun. The young people followed it and, once they had made their way to the large boulder, Anrus grabbed the red egg and touched the stone with it. The stone slid aside, and they made their way out of the land of the *phuvuša.* They then raced like the wind and threw the black egg into the river. The earth shook so strongly after they had done this that they lost their balance and fell to the ground. "Now, the *phuvuš* is dead!"* exclaimed Anrus.

What a celebration was held when they were back in the cabin of the poor man! Anrus and the beautiful young woman married and lived a life of joy and good fortune. On their wedding day, for the first time in seven years, the poor man began to laugh again.

📖 Wlislocki, *Volksdichtungen,* no. 14.†

---

*In several regions of Transylvania and Hungary the Gypsies call earthquakes "the death of the *phuvuš.*"

†[The footnotes are from Wlislocki's original texts. —*Trans.*]

APPENDIX

INDEX OF MOTIFS

The motifs indicated refer to the entries of the dictionary.

Amulet: Phallus
Animal Psychopomp: White Dog
Apple: Moon
Bone of a Hanged Man: Datura, Magical Conception
Brooklet of Wine: Leila
Broom: Hazel Tree
Cake: Poreskoro
Charm: Mašurdalo, Pçuvuš, Thread of the Virgin
Conjuration: Pharavono
Dream: Ašami
Egg: Ant, Blessed Mountains, Čarana, Cuckoo, Engagement, Lark, Lightning, Magic Conception, Nivaši, Owl, Pçuvuš, Snail, Snake, Urme, Water Lily, Worm of Good Fortune
Expulsion of Winter: King of the Shadows
Fish Girl: Lili
Flute: King Moon, King Sun, Magical Object, Moon
Flying Carpet: King Moon
Funeral Ritual: Revenant
Gastrotomy: Snake

Twins: Gypsy, Urme
Urine, Urination: Čarana, Dog-Man, Garlic, Loçolico
Voyage to the Other World: Other World
Wall of Iron: Mountain of the Cats
Water of Strength: Ana
Water Spirit: Bimuyakro, Ox
Worm of Madness: Rainbow

BIBLIOGRAPHY

Aichele, Walther. *Zigeunermärchen*. Jena: Diederichs, 1926.

Angold, F. H. "The Gypsy Approach to the Basic Opposites of Good and Evil." *Journal of the Gypsy Lore Society*. 3rd series, vol. 35 (1956): 154–61.

Benfey, Theodor. *Pantschatantra: Fünf Bücher indischer Fabeln, Märchen und Erzählungen*. Leipzig: Brockhaus, 1859.

Berge, François. "Les Bohémiens-Caraques et leur Terre Sainte de Camargue (Le pèlerinage des Saintes-Maries-de-la-Mer)." *Revue de l'histoire des religions* 85 (1920): 26–54.

Berger, Hermann. "Mythologie der Zigeuner." In Hans Wilhelm Haussig, ed., *Götter und mythen des indischen Subkontinents*. Stuttgart: Klett-Cotta, 1984. Pp. 773–824.

Bloch, Jules. *Les Tsiganes*. Paris: P.U.F., 1953.

Block, Martin. *Mœurs et Coutumes des Tsiganes*. Paris: Payot, 1936.

———. *Die materielle Kultur der rumänischen Zigeuner: Versuch einer monographischen Darstellung*. Frankfurt am Main: Lang, 1991.

———. *Die Zigeuner: Ihr Leben und ihre Seele dargestellt auf Grund eigener Reisen und Forschungen*. Frankfurt am Main: Lang, 1997.

Bonnefoy, Yves, ed. *Roman and European Mythologies*. Chicago: University of Chicago Press, 1992.

Bordigoni, Marc. *Gitans, Tsiganes, Roms . . . : idées reçues sur le monde du Voyage*. Paris: Le Cavalier Bleu, 2013.

Brednich, Rolf Wilhelm. "Les sources folkloriques du roman tsigane: *Les Ursitory* de Mateo Maximoff." *Études tsiganes* 9 (1963): 5–16.

Buckland, Raymond. *Book of Gypsy Magic: Travelers' Stories, Spells, & Healings*. San Francisco: Red Wheel/Weiser, 2010.

Carnoy, Henry, and Jean Nicolaïdes. *Folklore de Constantinople*. Paris: Lechavalier, 1894.

Clébert, Jean-Paul. *Les Tsiganes*. Paris: Arthaud, 1961.

Contes d'un Tzigane hongrois: János Berki raconte. Collected and presented by Veronika Görög-Karady. Paris: CNRS, 1991.

Cozannet, Françoise. *Mythes et Coutumes religieuses des Tsiganes*. Paris: Payot, 1973.

Delage, André. "Les Saintes-Maries-de-la-Mer: Des origines de la tradition des Saintes à nos jours." *Études tsiganes* 2, no. 4 (1956): 3–30.

Dictionnaire tchèque-tzigane et tzigane-tchèque. Kutná Hora: N.p., 1886.

Djordjević, Trgjić. "Erzählungen moslimischer Zigeuner aus dem Moravagebiete in Serbien." *Anthropophyteia* 2 (1905): 154–56.

Dollé, Marie-Paul. "Symbolique de la mort en milieu tsigane." *Études tsiganes* 4 (1970): 4–15.

Druts, E., and A. Gessler. *Skazki i pesni tsygan Rossii*. Moscow: Pravda, 1987.

Dyrlund, Folner. *Tatere og Natmandsfolk i Danmark: Betragtede med hensyn til samfundsforholdene i det hele*. Copenhagen: Gyldendal, 1872.

Erdös, C. "La notion de *mulo* ou mort-vivant et le culte des morts chez les Tsiganes hongrois." *Études tsiganes* 5:1 (1959): 1–9.

Erzherzog, Joseph. "Tiere im Glauben der Zigeuner." *Ethnologische Mitteilungen aus Ungarn* 4 (1895): 50–51.

Etzel, Anton von. *Vagabondenthum und Wanderleben in Norwegen*. Berlin: Heymann, 1870.

Fassel, Horst. "Heinrich Wlislocki, der bekannte Zigeunerforscher (1856–1907), Student in Klausenburg." *Studio Germanica Napocensia* 2 (2010): 301–17. [Contains a complete bibliography of Wlislocki's books and articles.]

Ficowski, Jerzy. *Gałązka z Drzewa Słońca*. Warsaw: Reader, 1961.

———. *Le Rameau de l'arbre du soleil, contes tziganes polonais d'après la tradition orale*. Châteauneuf: Wallâda, 1990.

Finck, Franz Nikolaus. *Lehrbuch des Dialekts der deutschen Zigeuner*. Marburg: Elwert, 1903.

Gerard, Emily. *The Land beyond the Forest: Facts, Figures, and Fancies from Transylvania*. New York: Harper & Brothers, 1888.

Gila-Kochanowski, Vania de. *Les Romané Chavé par eux-mêmes*.

Vol. 1: *Le roi des serpents et autres contes tsiganes balto-slaves*. Châteauneuf-les-Martigues: Wallâda, 1996.

Görög-Karady, Veronika, ed. "Problèmes d'identité et récits de création hongrois sur l'origine des Tsiganes." In M. M. J. Fernandez-Vest, ed. *Kalevala et Tradition orale du monde*. Paris: CNRS, 1987. Pp. 399–409.

———. *Contes d'un Tzigane hongrois. János Berki raconte*. Paris: CNRS, 1991

———. "Le statut du folklore et de la culture populaire tsiganes en Hongrie." *Études tsiganes* 2 (1994): 63–82.

Greimas, Algirdas Julien. *Of Gods and Men: Studies in Lithuanian Mythology*. Bloomington: University of Indiana Press, 1992.

Grimm, Jacob. *Deutsche mythologie*. 3 vols. Berlin: Dümmler, 1875.

Groome, Francis H. *Gypsy Folk-Tales*. London: Harstand Blackett, 1899.

———. *Gypsies, Tinkers and Other Travellers*. London: Academic Press, 1975.

Gruel-Apert, Lise. *Le Monde mythologique russe*. Paris: Imago, 2014.

Hahn, J. von. *Griechische und albanesische marchen*. 2 vols. Munich, Berlin: Muller, 1918.

Haltrich, Josef. *Zur Volkkunde der siebenbürgischen Sachsen*. Vienna: Graeser, 1885.

Heister, Carl von. *Ethnographische und geschichtliche Notizen über die Zigeuner*. Königsberg: Gräfe und Unzer, 1842.

Herrmann, Anton. *Märchen und Lieder der Roma*. Frankfurt, Berlin, New York: Lang, 1999.

Iversen, Ragnvald. *Secret Languages in Norway*. Part 1. *The Romany Language in Norway*. Oslo: Dybwad, 1944.

Ješina, P. Josef. *Románci čib oder die Zigeuner-Sprache* (Grammatik, Wörterbuch, Chrestomathie). 3rd expanded edition; 1st German edition. Leipzig: List & Francke, 1886.

———. *Slovník česko-cikánský a cikánsko-český jakož i cikánsko-české pohádky a povídky*. Kutná Hora: Šolce, 1889.

Johansson, Roger, Gösta Bergman, and Erik Ljungberg. *Svensk rommani*. Uppsala: Lundequistska Bokhandeln, 1977.

Kabakova, Galina, and Anna Stroeva. *Contes et légendes tsiganes*. Paris: Flies France, 2010.

Kalina, Antoine. *La Langue des Tsiganes slovaques*. Posen: Zupanski, 1882.

Karpati, Mirella. "Il mito cosmogonico degli Zingari Kalderaša." *Lacio Drom* 6 (1971): 29–35.

Kenrick, Donald, and D. Golemanov. "Three Gypsy Tales from the Balkans." *Folklore* 78/1 (1967): 59–60.

Knobloch, Johann. "Gypsy Tales concerning the 'Mulo.'" Translated by Bernard Gilliat-Smith. *Journal of the Gypsy Lore Society,* 3rd series, vol. 32 (1953): 124–32.

Kogalnitchan, Mihail de. *Esquisse sur l'histoire, les mœurs et la langue des Cigains connus en France sous le nom de Bohémiens.* Berlin: Behr, 1837.

Kornel, Vladislav. "Gypsy Anecdotes from Hungary." *Journal of the Gypsy Lore Society* 2 (1890): 65–73.

Krauss, Friedrich S. *Zigeunerhumor: 250 Schurren und Schwänke.* Leipzig: N.p., 1907.

Lecouteux, Claude. *Mélusine et le Chevalier au cygne.* Paris: Imago, 1997.

———. *Witches, Werewolves, and Fairies: Shapeshifters and Astral Doubles in the Middle Ages.* Translated by Clare Frock. Rochester, Vt.: Inner Traditions, 2006. [English edition of *Fées, Sorcières et loups-garous au Moyen Âge.*]

———. *Phantom Armies of the Night: The Wild Hunt and the Ghostly Processions of the Dead.* Translated into English by Jon E. Graham. Rochester, Vt.: Inner Traditions, 2011. [English edition of *Chasses infernales et Cohortes de la nuit.*]

———. *A Lapidary of Sacred Stones.* Translated by Jon E. Graham. Rochester, Vt.: Inner Traditions, 2011. [English edition of *Dictionnaire des pierres magiques et médicinales.*]

———. *The Tradition of Household Spirits: Ancestral Lore and Practices.* Translated by Jon E. Graham. Rochester, Vt.: Inner Traditions, 2013. [English edition of *La Maison et ses genies.*]

———. *Encyclopedia of Norse and Germanic Folklore, Mythology, and Magic.* Translated by Jon E. Graham. Edited by Michael Moynihan. Rochester, Vt.: Inner Traditions, 2016. [English edition of *Dictionnaire de mythologie germanique.*]

Leland, Charles Godfrey. *The English Gipsies and Their Language.* London: Trübner, 1874.

———. *The Gypsies.* Boston: Houghton, Mifflin and Co., 1882.

———. *Gypsy Sorcery and Fortune Telling.* London: Fisher Unwin, 1891.

Liebich, Richard. *Die Zigeuner in ihrem Wesen und in ihrer Sprache.*

Nach eigenen Beobachtungen dargestellt. Leipzig: Brockhaus, 1863.

Martinez, Nicole. "Du 'mulo' tsigane au 'mujao' andalou: Invariant culturel ou histoire d'un envoûtement collectif?" In *Les cahiers de l'imaginaire,* vol. 10: *Rencontres et apparitions fantastiques.* Paris: L'Harmattan, 1994.

Marushiakova, Elena, and Vesselin Popov. "Legends." In Marushiakova and Vesselin, eds. *Studii romani,* vol. II. Sofia: Club 90, 1995. Pp. 22–45.

Matras, Yaron. *Romani: A Linguistic Introduction.* Cambridge: Cambridge University Press, 2002.

Maximoff, Matéo. *Les Ursitory.* Paris: Flammarion, 1946.

Meltzl, Hugo. "Literatur als weltbewegende Größe." *Studio Germanica Napocensia* 2 (2010): 105–42.

Michaelis, Wilhelm. *Die apokryphen Schriften zum Neuen Testament.* Bremen: Schunemann, 1958.

Miklosich, Franz. *Über die Mundarten und die Wanderungen der Zigeuner Europa's.* Vienna: Karl Gerold's Sohn, 1872.

Mingot-Tauran, Françoise. "Éditer la parole tzigane. L'expérience de Wallâda." *Études tsiganes* 37 (2009): 130–72.

Nagy, Olga. "The Persistence of Archaic Traits among Gypsy Storytelling Communities in Romania." *Journal of the Gypsy Lore Society,* 4th series, vol. 1 (1978): 221–39.

Nounev, Yosif. "Legends." *Studii Romani* 1 (1994): 48–61.

Obert, Franz. *Rumänische Märchen und Sagen aus Siebenbürgen.* Hermannstadt: Krafft, 1925.

Oişteanu, Andrei. "The Romanian Legend of the Flood." *Archæus* IV (2000): 69–103.

Pabanó, F. M. (Félix Manzano López). *Historia y costumbres de los gitanos. Collección deentos viejos y nuevos, dichos y timos graciosos, maldiciones y refranes netamente gitanos. Diccionario español-gitano-germanesco, dialecto de los gitanos.* Barcelona: Montaner y Simón, 1915.

Patrut, Iulia-Karin. "Wlislocki's Transylvanian 'Gypsies' and the Discourses on Aryanism around 1900." *Romani Studies* 17/2 (Dec. 2007): 181–204.

Paspati, Alexandre G. *Études sur les Tchinghaniés ou Bohémiens de l'empire ottoman.* Constantinople: Koroméla, 1870.

Payne, Charles F. "Some Romani Superstitions." *Journal of the Gypsy Lore Society,* 3rd series, vol. 36 (1957): 110–15.

Rehfisch, F., ed. *Gypsies, Tinkers and Other Travellers.* London: Academic Press, 1975.

Ros', Jangil. *Voyage maison.* Paris: Publibook, 2008.

Schwicker, Johann Heinrich. *Die Zigeuner in Ungarn und Siebenbürgen.* Vienna & Teschen: Prochaska, 1883.

Serboianu, Popp. *Les Tziganes.* Paris: Payot, 1930.

Stoichita, Victor Alexandre. *Fabricants d'émotion: Musique et malice dans un village tsigane de roumanie.* Paris: Société d'ethnologie, 2008.

Taloş, Ion. *Gândirea magico-religioasă la români: Dicţionar.* Bucharest: Editura Enciclopedică, 2001.

Tillhagen, Carl Hermann. *Zigeunermärchen und -geschichten.* Zurich: Artemis, 1948.

Thomasius, Jacob. *Dissertatio philosophica de cingaris.* Leipzig: Hahn, 1671.

Uerlings, Herbert, and Iulia-Karin Patrut, eds. *Zigeuner und Nation.* Frankfurt: Lang, 2008.

Vaillant, Jean-Alexandre. *Grammaire, Dialogues et Vocabulaire de la Langue des Bohémiens ou Cigains.* Paris: Maisonneuve, 1868.

Ville, Frans de. *Tziganes, témoins des temps.* Brussels: Office de Publicité, 1956.

Willman-Grabowska, Helena. "Le chien dans l'*Avesta* et dans les *Védas.*" *Polskie towarzystwo Orjentalistyczne* (1934): 30–67.

Vukanović, T. P. "The Vampire in Belief and Customs of the Gypsies in the Province of Kosovo-Metohija, Stari Ras and Novopazarski Sandžak, Yugoslavia." *Journal of the Gypsy Lore Society,* 3rd series, vol. 36 (1957): 125–33; vol. 37 (1958): 21–31, 111–19; vol. 38 (1959): 44–55.

Wlislocki, Heinrich von. *Die Sprache der transsilvanischen Zigeuner: Grammatik, Wörterbuch.* Leipzig: Friedrich, 1884.

———. "Zur Volkskunde der transsilvanischen Zigeuner." *Ungarische Revue,* issue 4 (1884): 229–58.

———. *Märchen und Sagen der transsilvanischen Zigeuner.* Berlin: Nicolai, 1886.

———. "Gebräuche der transsilvanischen Zigeuner bei Geburt, Taufe und Leichenbestattung." *Globus, Illustrierte Zeitschrift für Länder- und Völkerkunde* 51 (1887): 249–51, 267–70.

———. *Zur Volkskunde der transsilvanischen Zigeuner.* Hamburg: Richter, 1887.

———. *Zauber- und Besprechungsformeln der transsilvanischen und südungarischen Zigeuner.* Extracted from Ethnologische Mitteilungen aus Ungarn, vol. 1, issues 1 and 2. Budapest: 1887–1888.

———. *Volksdichtungen der siebenbürgischen und südungarischen Zigeuner.* Vienna: Graeser, 1890.

———. *Vom wandernden Zigeunervolke: Bilder aus dem Leben der Siebenbürger Zigeuner, Geschichtliches, Ethnologisches, Sprache und Poesie.* Hamburg: Actien-Gesellschaft, 1890.

———. "Urmen: Schicksalsfrauen der Zigeuner." *Am Ur-Quell, Monatschrift für Volkskunde* 2 (1891): 133–36.

———. *Volksglaube und religiöser Brauch der Zigeuner.* Münster I. W.: Aschendorff, 1891.

———. "The Witch of the Gypsies." *Journal of the Gypsy Lore Society* 3 (1891–1892): 38–45.

———. "The Worship of the Mountains among the Gypsies." *Journal of the Gypsy Lore Society* 3 (1891–1892): 161–69, 211–19.

———. *Volksglaube und religiöser Brauch der Magyaren.* Münster I. W.: Aschendorff, 1893.

———. "Quälgeister im Volksglauben der Rumänen." *Am Ur-Quell, Monatschrift für Volkskunde* 6 (1896): 17–19, 60–62, 90–92, 108–110, 142–44.

———. *La Rose et le Musicien: Contes tziganes.* Translated by Claude and Corinne Lecouteux. Paris: Corti, 2016.

Wittich, Engelbert. *Blicke in das Leben der Zigeuner.* Striegau: Huß, 1911.

Wratislaw, Graf von, and Rudolf Mitrovic. *Versuch einer Darstellung der Lebensweise, Herkunft und Sprache der Zigeuner im Allgemeinen und der in Österreich lebenden Zigeuner insbesondere.* Prague: Mercy, 1868.

Zanko, chef tribal chez les Chalderash. La tradition des Tsiganes conservée par l'aristocratie de ce peuple: Le "Livre des ancêtres." Le coutumier. La mise à mort du serpent. Les legends. Documents collected by the Reverend Father Chatard, presented by Michel Bernard. Paris: La Colombe, 1959.

BOOKS OF RELATED INTEREST

Traditional Magic Spells for Protection and Healing
by Claude Lecouteux

Encyclopedia of Norse and Germanic Folklore, Mythology, and Magic
by Claude Lecouteux

Dictionary of Ancient Magic Words and Spells
From Abraxas to Zoar
by Claude Lecouteux

The Hidden History of Elves and Dwarfs
Avatars of Invisible Realms
by Claude Lecouteux
Foreword by Régis Boyer

The Tradition of Household Spirits
Ancestral Lore and Practices
by Claude Lecouteux

The Book of Grimoires
The Secret Grammar of Magic
by Claude Lecouteux

Demons and Spirits of the Land
Ancestral Lore and Practices
by Claude Lecouteux

A Lapidary of Sacred Stones
Their Magical and Medicinal Powers Based on the Earliest Sources
by Claude Lecouteux

INNER TRADITIONS • BEAR & COMPANY
P.O. Box 388
Rochester, VT 05767
1-800-246-8648
www.InnerTraditions.com

Or contact your local bookseller